MW00803183

HMH | English 3D™

ISSUES

COURSE B • VOLUME 1

Copyright © by Houghton Mifflin Harcourt Publishing Company

All rights reserved. No part of this work may be reproduced or transmitted in any form or by any means, electronic or mechanical, including photocopying or recording, or by any information storage or retrieval system, without the prior written permission of the copyright owner unless such copying is expressly permitted by federal copyright law. Requests for permission to make copies of any part of the work should be submitted through our Permissions website at https://customercare.hmhco.com/contactus/Permissions.html or mailed to Houghton Mifflin Harcourt Publishing Company, Attn: Compliance, Contracts, and Licensing, 9400 Southpark Center Loop, Orlando, Florida 32819-8647.

Printed in the U.S.A.

ISBN 978-0-358-60951-3

6   7   8   9   10   0607   29 28 27 26 25 24 23 22

4500861617   r10.21

If you have received these materials as examination copies free of charge, Houghton Mifflin Harcourt Publishing Company retains title to the materials, and they may not be resold. Resale of examination copies is strictly prohibited.

Possession of this publication in print format does not entitle users to convert this publication, or any portion of it, into electronic format.

TABLE OF **CONTENTS**

Academic Words in *Issues* Texts

Words to Go and Concept Words: High-utility words that you will encounter in other texts and content areas are **highlighted in yellow**.

Words to Know: Topic-related words that you can use to discuss and write about the Issue are **boldface**.

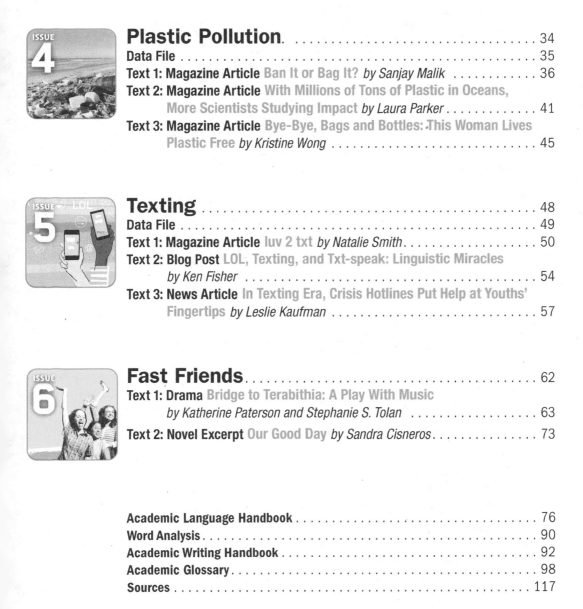

CAN **VIDEO GAMES** TAKE YOUR **BRAIN** TO THE NEXT **LEVEL?**

Video games have come a long way from the simple ping-pong games of the 1980s. Now you can fight zombies, quarterback football teams, or float flappy birds from a cell phone.

Video games can be fun, but are they also harmful? Some people worry about how video games affect young players. Do they make it harder to pay attention? What about bloody images?

Other people point out that video games can teach players to solve problems. They can also develop muscle movements and help people make friends.

Do video games prepare people for life, or shut them off from it? Do they help or hurt your brain? Press "start" to find out!

Data File

Since video games started coming into homes in the 1980s, their complexity and popularity keep reaching new levels.

Powering Up

Teens play video games on consoles, computers, handheld devices, and cell phones.

- According to a survey, **97%** of teens aged 12–17 play video games.
- By gender, **99%** of boys and **94%** of girls enjoy this form of entertainment.
- **65%** of game-playing teens play **socially** with other people who are in the same room. **24%** of teens only play video games online.

(Pew Research Center, 2008)

MATURE
17+

Mature Enough?

Video game ratings include E = Everyone, E10+ = Everyone 10+, T = Teen, and M = Mature. Of the 40 best-selling computer and video games in 2013, T was the most common rating with 16 games. M-rated games are the most controversial because they contain strong language, intense violence, and other adult content.

(Entertainment Software Association, 2014)

Out of Control

While video games are a fun activity for most players, they take over some players' lives.

- Research shows that nearly **10%** of gamers are **addicted**.
- **Addicted** teens play video games about **24** hours per week. Some play many hours more.

(Psychological Science, 2009)

Game On or Game Over?

by Oscar Gomez

Brian Alegre thought he was in control—until a video game took over his life. "I had this big urge to play all the time," he said. That urge built up to 15–20 hours of play a day. Alegre guzzled energy drinks. He started to mix up his virtual world and RL, or "real life." Brian had to face a harsh fact. He was an **addict**.

Not all players experience the dark side of video games. Michael Chaves is a professional video gamer. He thinks gaming has made him function better in real life. "I'm always thinking because in the game, you are trying to accomplish certain tasks. And if I could do it in the game, I feel I can do it in person, too."

Opinions about video games are intense. On one side, people think the games are great entertainment. They say, "Game on." On the other side, people think video games are **violent** and **addictive**. They say, "Game over."

Mind Games

"I don't think playing video games really affects kids that much," Parker Seagren says. Seagren, a teen from Illinois, plays war and sports games with his friends. Many teens would agree with Seagren. For them, video games are just part of life. And that life includes 24/7 technology. Parents and other adults just don't get it. After all,

According to the Pew Research Center, 94% of teen girls play video games.

they grew up in another century. However, scientists know that video games do affect teens. They have gathered evidence about how video games **influence** the brain. When it experiences something pleasurable, the brain releases a chemical called dopamine. As a result, the brain is hard-wired to want more of that thing. It wants to press "Play Again."

About 8.5 percent of teen gamers develop an addiction to video games. They are more likely to skip school, receive poor grades, and have social problems.

Brain studies help explain why about 8.5 percent of teen gamers develop an **addiction** to video games. They are more likely to skip school, receive poor grades, and have **social** problems. These facts create a powerful argument against video games.

However, people in favor of video games also cite brain studies. They contain evidence that shows the positive **influence** of video games. For example, experiments show that action video games affect parts of the brain that control vision and coordination. As a result, video games can improve the ability to pilot an aircraft, read X-rays, and perform surgery. Supporters also argue that video games make players active problem solvers. Players have to think of better ways to advance in their games.

Video games can help improve the skills pilots use to fly aircraft.

Winners or Losers?

"Video games are ruining my life," says one high school student who is **addicted** to online games. "If I'm not playing, I'm thinking about playing. I have, like, no real friends."

Some teens spend more time with video games than with friends. Critics say that video games can distract young people from real life. If teens are already having problems, games allow them to escape into a fantasy world. Once that happens, it is difficult for some to land back in reality.

Supporters of video games disagree that video game players are **antisocial** loners. They say it is an exaggerated stereotype. A survey by the Pew Internet and American Life Project backs up their argument. The survey shows that gaming is often a **beneficial social** experience for teens. More than half of teens play **interactive** video games with other people who are in the same room. The players work as a team. They solve problems as a group. In fact, the games **benefit** players' **social** skills rather than harm them.

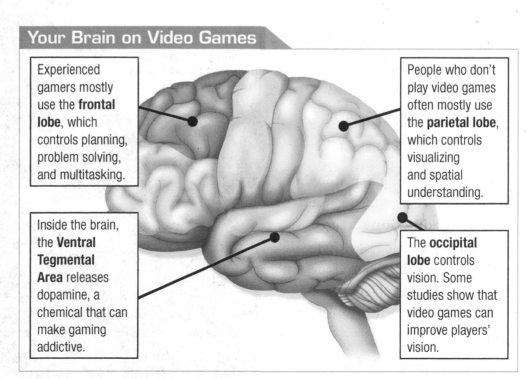

Your Brain on Video Games

Experienced gamers mostly use the **frontal lobe**, which controls planning, problem solving, and multitasking.

People who don't play video games often mostly use the **parietal lobe**, which controls visualizing and spatial understanding.

Inside the brain, the **Ventral Tegmental Area** releases dopamine, a chemical that can make gaming addictive.

The **occipital lobe** controls vision. Some studies show that video games can improve players' vision.

More than half
of teens play
interactive
video games with
other people
who are in
the same room.
The players work
as a team. They
solve problems
as a group.

Many teens play games that have positive effects. However, other teens are sucked into the world of action and first-person shooter games. It can be a world where video **violence** rules.

Combat Zone

Video game **violence** is a hot-button **issue**. Some games contain extreme **violence**. That stirs up extreme emotions. These games are rated for Mature or Adult audiences. However, many teens spend significant amounts of time playing them.

Surveys show that playing video games with others can have social benefits.

On the steps of the US Supreme Court, protestors rallied against a California law banning the sale of violent video games to minors.

Both boys and girls who play M-rated games get in fights and damage property more often than teens who don't play M-rated games.

California passed a law in 2005 that banned the sale of **violent** video games to minors. Governor Arnold Schwarzenegger said that California had a responsibility to protect children from "the effects of games that depict ultra-**violent** actions." In 2011, the US Supreme Court struck down the law. The court ruled that the law violated the First Amendment, which protects freedom of speech.

Critics of the games argue that teens transfer the **violence** they see to the real world. In fact, studies have shown that the games can be negative **influences**. Both boys and girls who play M-rated games get in fights and damage property more often than teens who don't play M-rated games.

Researchers have also tested the effects of the games on teens' brains. The findings show that **violent** games have significant short-term effects. They raise aggression and lower self-control. However, experts point out that a small amount of video game **violence** isn't going to turn a normal teen into a criminal.

How can you know when someone's gaming is becoming a problem? Warning signs include lying about playing, withdrawing **socially**, and neglecting schoolwork. The worst sign is confusing games with real life.

No matter where people stand on the **issue**, they all agree that video games can have incredible power over players.

Technology ⟩ CONTENT CONNECTION

Video Games to the Rescue

Disasters usually strike with little or no warning. When they happen, emergency workers need to think clearly, act fast, and work in coordination with each other. How can disaster workers train for their dangerous jobs? Video games come to the rescue.

Video games can simulate disasters such as fires, chemical spills, explosions, and hurricanes. While playing the games, emergency workers learn to make decisions and solve problems. They plot escape routes, defuse bombs, organize rescues, and provide medical attention. The games prepare them for disasters in the real world.

Take a Stand

If you could create a video game to prepare responders for one of these disasters, which would you choose? Why?

1. earthquake
2. terrorist bomb in an airport
3. electricity blackout

New Study Links Video Gaming to Creativity

by Elizabeth Armstrong Moore

For those who like to play video games, or who let their kids play, a new study linking gaming to **creativity** in 12-year-olds may be very validating.

The research comes out of Michigan State University and was published online in the journal *Computers in Human Behavior*. It found that of the 491 12-year-olds studied, the ones who play video games tend to be more **creative**. This is regardless of whether those games are **violent** or not. In fact, the more video games they play, the more **creative** these 12-year-olds are.

The head researcher of this study is psychology professor Linda Jackson. She says these findings should encourage game designers to investigate which parts of gaming are more responsible for making kids more **creative**.

"Once they do that, video games can be designed to optimize the development of **creativity**," she says in a news release. At the same time, they can keep their entertainment factor. The result? A new generation of video games that will blur the line between education and entertainment!

But before we exchange those dusty books for video games, let's look more closely at a few parts of the study.

First, there is the **issue** of how **creativity** is measured. Measuring technology use for this study was easy. Jackson's team relied on the Torrance Tests of Creative Thinking.

Researchers hope game designers can find out which parts of games make players more creative.

This involved having the kids perform tasks such as drawing pictures from a curved shape, then naming and writing stories about those pictures.

Some of the resulting work was labeled "interesting and exciting." Other work was not. So what does this tell us? That kids who play video games meet one set of criteria for **creativity** more than kids who don't.

Even if **creativity** is an objective quality, this one measure for it might not sufficiently determine one's overall **creativity**. It risks ignoring other types of **creativity** altogether. For example, one kid might be able to draw **creatively**, while another can make up new songs **creatively**, so only measuring the drawing could result in missing other forms of **creativity**.

And then there is the **issue** of what is being compared. Instead of measuring one type of activity against another, this study measures one type against the absence of it. This leaves a lot of room for variables. Are the kids who don't play video games watching TV? How would the group playing video games compare to kids building their own puzzles? Or

The Michigan State study measured creativity by having children draw pictures and write stories. However, people can be creative in many ways.

kids making mud pies? Or kids drawing pictures from a curved shape and then naming and writing stories about those pictures?

Even if creativity is an objective quality, this one measure for it might not sufficiently determine one's overall creativity.

This study may be the first of many to come. For now, I'll continue enjoying video games, with the added pleasure of knowing that I might possibly be maximizing my **creativity**. Of course, whether it's working will depend upon whom you ask.

Debate — Does school food make the grade?

French fries or steamed veggies? Pizza or grilled chicken? A cupcake or a fruit salad?

All these small decisions add up. What people eat affects their health. Many Americans, including many children, are overweight.

Some people believe school lunches are part of the problem. In 2012, the government changed the rules for school lunches. The rules say schools have to serve more fruits and vegetables. They also call for less salt and fat.

How much choice should students have about what they eat? What should school cafeterias serve? Let's look at lunch!

Data File

American students are facing a health crisis. Is school food part of the problem? Or is it part of the solution?

A Health Crisis

Obesity can harm people's health. It can lead to diabetes, heart disease, and other serious illnesses. Recent studies show that one in three American children and teens is overweight or **obese**. This rate has tripled in the last 50 years.

(American Heart Association, 2014)

Food by the Numbers

- More than 30 million students eat school lunches every day. That adds up to 150 million trays of cafeteria food per week.

- The government has **nutritional** standards for school lunches. For example, middle school lunches must have 600–700 **calories**.

(US Department of Agriculture Food and Nutrition Service, 2014)

Snacks for Sale

- In 2010, vending machines were in 52% of middle schools and 88% of high schools. Using vending machines can be an **expensive habit**. A student can spend up to $10 a week on vending machine food.

- About 22% of students from elementary school to high school buy food in vending machines every day. The food adds an average of 253 **calories** per day to each student's diet.

(Journal of School Health, 2010)

Food Fight

by Dora Rodriguez

How do teens feel about junk food in school? Opinions range from pro-junk food to pro-health food.

"We're teenagers. We don't want healthy food," explains Kaleb Lewis, a teen from Portland, Oregon.

"I'm a quarterback on the football team," says Kayron Evans from New York. "So I've got to stay healthy, got to get my arms strong." He takes **nutrition** seriously. He regularly eats salad with his lunch.

"Lunch for me is chips, soda, maybe a chocolate ice cream taco," says Nicole Talbott. She buys her lunch at a market near school.

Essence Crum avoids junk food. The track athlete from Tampa, Florida, says, "At practice, coach is always telling me, 'You need water, you need fruits and vegetables if you want to win the race.' That motivates me to eat right."

The war on junk food in schools started about a decade ago. That is when studies revealed the **epidemic** of **obesity** in young people. Soon, the government, schools, parents, and students took sides on the issue. The food fight still goes on. Your body is the battleground.

Some teens regularly make healthy snack choices.

➊ NO to Junk Food in School

First Lady Michelle Obama admits that she loves burgers, fries, ice cream, and cake. However, she adds, "The problem is when that fun stuff becomes the **habit**. And I think that's what's happened in our culture. Fast food has become the everyday meal."

Mrs. Obama wants to **prevent** childhood **obesity**. She believes serving **nutritious** food in schools would help achieve that goal.

> **Snacking on junk food in school adds up to about 14 extra pounds per child per school year.**

The federal government will not fund junk food as part of school lunch. Since 2014, schools can no longer sell candy bars, soda, potato chips, and other high-fat snack foods in vending machines. Many people support the new guidelines. One teacher says, "The message we send by having all these deals with junk-food peddlers is that this stuff is okay." Studies **indicate** that snacking on junk food in school adds up to about 14 extra pounds per child per school year.

California is a leader in the **prevention** of childhood **obesity**. It was one of the first states to ban junk food in public schools. A recent study shows that the policy has been beneficial. Within three years, the **trend** of overweight students decreased. Education about healthy eating also helped. "Kids have no idea what a **calorie** is," says Zenobia Barlow, a California-based educator. "But when they're told they'll have to run six laps to work off a bag of chips, it starts to change behaviors."

➋ YES to Junk Food in School

Many people are against **banning** junk food in schools. They want to make all food choices **available** to students. John Dively, Executive Director of the Illinois Principals Association, says this: "An across-the-board junk-food **ban** does not teach young people how to make healthy choices. It simply removes some of their options."

For many students, school vending machines are an **appealing** option. The most popular vending machine items used to include candy, chips, crackers, cookies, cakes, and soft drinks. Many students use vending machine food to tide them over between lunch and dinner.

Eddie Livesay, a student from Tampa, Florida, says, "The people who go to the vending machines are the ones that have sports after school or other activities. They need the extra energy to survive the day."

Food sales also have a major financial **impact** for many schools. They use the money to buy **expensive** equipment for sports teams and other clubs.

"Being 18, technically I can be drafted into the military. But I'm not allowed to have snacks at school. That doesn't make sense."

MyPlate Guidelines for Americans

Fruits

Grains

Dairy

Vegetables

Protein

ChooseMyPlate.gov

Source: US Department of Agriculture, 2010

Fresh fruit is available in this middle school cafeteria line.

At Orange County High School in Virginia, a candy cart appeared in hallways three times a day. The cart netted about $400 to $500 a week from candy sales.

In Texas, eight schools were fined $73,000 for breaking a state law against junk-food fund-raisers in 2013. Later that year, a new law allowed high schools to continue the events.

❸ Who Decides?

Should you have the right to eat junk food in school? Whose decision should it be?

Richard Codey, former acting governor of New Jersey, believes it's the government's responsibility to **restrict** junk food at school. "It has always been the role of government to help solve problems, especially health crises. **Obesity** is a health **epidemic** across our country."

Others argue that a child learns eating **habits** at home, not at school. "My mom's always telling me I'm going to get diabetes by the time I'm 16," says one Oregon high school freshman. He admits that he just went out for a fast food lunch with his friends.

Many students say they have the right to **select** what they eat. Eddie Livesay puts it this way: "Being 18, technically I can be drafted into the military. But I'm not allowed to have snacks at school. That doesn't make sense."

Essence Crum doesn't think schools have to **restrict** all junk food. "If kids know what they're eating, know it's bad for them, know it's fatty food, I think they'd be more concerned about their weight." She believes teens will **select nutritious** food if they know the consequences.

What side of the debate are you on? Do teens need to be protected from junk food? Or can they learn to make their own healthy choices?

Health — CONTENT CONNECTION

Reading a Nutrition Label

How can you tell if a food is healthy or junk? Nutrition labels give information about serving size, calories, and nutrients.

1 Serving Size A serving size is an amount of food people typically eat. The nutrition facts apply to a single serving. If the serving size is half a cup, but you eat a full cup, you will consume twice the calories and nutrients listed.

2 Calories Calories measure how much energy you get from food. A teen male needs about 2,600 calories per day, and a teen female needs 2,200.

3 Nutrients Nutrients include the proteins, minerals, and vitamins that you need to stay healthy. The numbers tell how many grams of each nutrient are in a serving. Try to choose foods that are low in fat, cholesterol, sodium, and sugars.

Nutrition Facts

1 Serving Size ½ cup (114g)
Servings Per Container 4

Amount Per Serving

2 **Calories** 90   Calories from Fat 30

	% Daily Value*
Total Fat 3g	5%
Saturated Fat 0g	0%
Cholesterol 0g	0%
Sodium 300g	13%
Total Carbohydrate 13g	4%
Dietary Fiber 3g	12%
Sugars 3g	
Protein 3g	

Vitamin A 80%	•	Vitamin C 60%
Calcium 4%	•	Iron 4%

*Percent Daily Values are based on a 2,000 calorie diet. Your daily values may be higher or lower depending on your caloric needs.

Take a Stand

Should all restaurants be required to provide nutrition facts? Why or why not?

The First Lady Announces New School Wellness Standards

by Michelle Obama

See, Let's Move is based on a very simple idea that parents should be in control of their kids' health. And their good efforts at home shouldn't be undermined when they send their kids off to school. Parents have a right to expect that during the school day, their kids will have food that meets basic **nutrition** standards, and they'll have a chance to maybe move around a little bit while they're there, too.

And that's why we launched Let's Move Active Schools. And today, more than 6,500 schools are bringing physical activity back into the classrooms. And because of the child **nutrition** bill we passed back in 2010, today nearly 90 percent of our schools—90 percent of them— have already **implemented** new school lunch standards.

With the hard work of so many administrators and chefs, **nutrition** professionals, and others, these schools have literally transformed their menus. They're serving more fruits and veggies, more whole grains, and more lean protein. And starting next fall, they'll be offering only healthy snacks and beverages in their vending machines as well.

So this is a big deal. And so far, these changes have been a resounding success. In fact, in a number of American school districts—places like Dallas, Orlando, Cincinnati—although they're not charging any more for their lunches, they're actually making more money because more kids are participating in the school lunch programs.

> **"Because of the child nutrition bill we passed back in 2010, today nearly 90 percent of our schools have already implemented new school lunch standards."**

So we're making some real strides in our schools. And that's why I'm thrilled to continue this progress with two very important announcements we're making today.

The first is that we're issuing new school wellness guidelines to help build healthier learning environments for our kids. And as part of this effort, we'll be **eliminating** advertisements for unhealthy food and beverages in our schools. Because I think we can all agree that our classrooms should be healthy places where kids are not bombarded with ads for junk food.

And these new marketing guidelines are actually part of a broader effort to inspire companies to rethink how they market food to kids in general. Because the fact is, today, the average child watches thousands of food advertisements each year, and 86 percent of these ads are for products loaded with sugar, fat, or salt. And, by contrast, our kids see an average of just one ad a week for healthy products like water, fruits, and vegetables. Just one. So that's why we convened the first ever White House Summit on food marketing to children, where I urged businesses

First Lady Michelle Obama started the Let's Move campaign in 2010 to fight childhood obesity.

to stop marketing unhealthy foods to our kids and do more to get kids excited about healthy foods. And that same principle should apply to our schools.

Our second announcement today focuses on school breakfast, and I cannot possibly overstate how important this is, because right now, millions of children in this country are showing up for school hungry every day. And too many kids aren't eating breakfast even when it's provided because they feel like there's a stigma with participating in the school breakfast program. And this is happening here in the wealthiest country on Earth, and it's intolerable.

And that's why we're expanding our school breakfast program, ensuring that nearly 9 million kids in 22,000 schools start their day with a **nutritious** breakfast. And as you all know, this doesn't just affect their health, it affects their performance in school. In fact, a recent study showed that kids who eat a healthy breakfast perform 17.5 percent better on math tests, and they have fewer disciplinary problems.

The school breakfast program will help nine million students start their days with nutritious food.

So this is critical for our kids' future and it's also critical for the future of our country because healthy and well-educated kids are more likely to become healthy, well-educated adults who will build a productive workforce and a vibrant economy for generations to come.

> "Kids who eat a healthy breakfast perform 17.5 percent better on math tests, and they have fewer disciplinary problems."

Where's the line between art and vandalism?

When graffiti took off in the 1970s, few people thought it was art. The tags and drawings on city walls and subway cars were against the law, plain and simple. Graffiti often marked areas as being dangerous.

Graffiti has come a long way since then. Now, some neighborhoods ask graffiti artists to paint murals. Some graffiti artists even sell their work in fancy art galleries for thousands of dollars!

Who has it right? Is graffiti a genuine art form that requires talent? Or is it willful harm to someone else's property?

Some people love it. Some people hate it. Graffiti creates more controversy than almost any other kind of self-expression.

Graffiti Glossary

graffiti: unauthorized words or drawings that are painted, scratched, or scribbled	**throwups:** quickly done bubble letters or simple two-color pieces
piece: a complex, **artistic** work that requires skill and time	**tag:** a signature or logo
writer: someone who does **expressive** pieces	**tagger:** someone who only does tags and throwups

Who Does It?

- Most graffiti taggers are males between 12 and 21 years old. Approximately **15%** are female.
- About **80%** of graffiti is tagger graffiti. About **10%** is gang related.

(Keep America Beautiful, 2014)

$$$ What Are the Costs?

Getting rid of graffiti costs **communities** about $12 billion per year *(US Department of Justice, 2009)*. San Francisco alone spends more than $20 million a year *(S.F. Department of Public Works, 2014)*. Graffiti **artists** risk penalties such as **vandalism** charges, thousands of dollars in fines, and years in jail.

The Writing on the Wall

by Kim Nguyen

They work at night covering walls, buildings, and trains with graffiti. They call themselves **artists**. The police call them **vandals**. Who are they really?

The Manhattan graffiti **artist** Alain Maridueña uses the tag KET. He views himself as an **artist**. "Wealthy building owners think that having something on the wall hurts their property values and makes people fearful," Maridueña says. "(But) young people think that writing on the wall is a form of **expression**; it's **artistic**, and it's beautiful."

Khalid Shah is the director of Stop the Violence, a gang intervention program. He believes that graffiti is not just **vandalism**, but dangerous as well. Gangs use graffiti to mark their territory, which can lead to violence. "The cause for a lot of violence involves graffiti and either crossing it out or **removing** it," he said. For example, two young men were

Graffiti has influenced fashion, music, and other forms of art.

shot dead when **removing** graffiti from a wall in Los Angeles.

Graffiti has been part of American **culture** since the 1960s and 1970s. Taggers spray-painted their designs on New York City subway cars. The trend quickly moved to other cities and became part of the urban landscape. Over the past 50 years, graffiti has been called everything from street art to crime. The writing on the wall still generates intense opinions and **criticism**.

"Young people think that writing on the wall is a form of expression; it's artistic, and it's beautiful."

Graffiti Penalties in Selected States*

State	Maximum Jail Time	Maximum Fine	Other Penalties
California	1 year (3 years if a felony)	$1,000 ($10,000 if more than $400 in damage)	N/A
Florida	1 year (5 years if more than $1,000 in damage)	$1,000 ($5,000 if more than $1,000 in damage)	mandatory community service and minimum fine of $250 for first offense
New York	1 year	$1,000	N/A
Texas	6 months (1 year if more than $500 in damage)	$2,000 ($4,000 if more than $500 in damage)	N/A

*as of 2014

❶ It's a Crime

Graffiti **critics** often use the "broken windows theory" to explain their views. It goes like this. One broken window in a **community** encourages **vandals** to break more windows. Soon, the whole **community** becomes a **target** for littering, **vandalism**, and crime.

Richard Condon organized a major graffiti conference in Washington, DC. He thinks graffiti has an impact just like a broken window. "The neighborhood begins to deteriorate, and then that invites first minor crime and then major crime. We can see this in a lot of our cities where graffiti has just taken over."

According to the Los Angeles Police Department, gang graffiti affects **communities** even more. Gangs use graffiti to **represent** their power or to challenge rivals. It isn't just property that is being **defaced**. The people in a **community** can become victims as well. The LAPD website issues this warning:

"When a neighborhood is marked with graffiti indicating territorial dominance, the entire area and its inhabitants become **targets** for violence. Anyone in the street or in their home is fair game for drive-by attacks by rival gang members. . . . Consequently, innocent residents are often subjected to gang violence by the mere presence of graffiti in their neighborhood."

Gangs use graffiti to represent their power or to challenge rivals. It isn't just property that is being defaced.

❷ It's Street Art

Graffiti **artists** view themselves as rebels, not criminals. They believe their writing is a form of **artistic expression** and free speech. They claim that it makes a neighborhood beautiful and gives the **community** a **cultural identity.** For decades, the Mission District in San Francisco has been an open-air gallery for graffiti **artists** like Las Mujeres Muralistas, Barry McGee (Twist), and Juana Alicia. The Mission's graffiti appeals to tourists rather than driving them away.

A young San Francisco graffiti writer who goes by the name SAVZ is proud of his **identity** as a graffiti **artist**. "How many people can say they risk their lives, their freedom, and their well-being for their art? All graffiti writers can."

Another response to **criticism** of graffiti is that it is a victimless crime. Supporters claim that graffiti is a means of **expression** for people without money and power. It's a street **culture** that benefits a **community**. McGee puts it this way: "There's a lot of talk of how **damaging** graffiti

Murals in San Francisco's Mission District attract tourists.

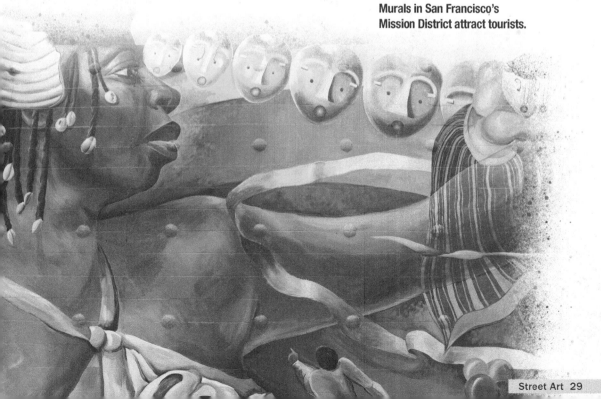

is . . . but there's actually no **damage**. It all can be **removed** or painted over with a roller." McGee compares graffiti to the commercial advertisements that cover walls and billboards all over the country. His **critique** is that graffiti is art, but billboards just sell things. He says people with money can put their messages everywhere without punishment. Meanwhile, graffiti **artists** are prevented from **expressing** themselves.

❸ Drawing the Line

In many cities, graffiti has become a **political** issue. **Politicians** are trying to draw the line between graffiti as art and graffiti as crime. In San Diego, the police are going after graffiti offenders like never before. But San Diego graffiti **artist** Josh Peterson (Kroer) protests that the punishment does not match the crime. He **interprets** his writing as art, not crime. "It's not like we're going out and robbing a store, or harming kids, or selling

Barry McGee (Twist) is a graffiti artist who has a degree in painting and printmaking from the San Francisco Art Institute.

drugs," he says. "It's putting art on gray buildings."

Bill Miles from the San Diego County Sheriff's office says gang graffiti differs from **artistic** graffiti. "Now, the difference between taggers and gangsters is that some taggers go by themselves, they're 'oners.' They have no affiliation with a crew or anything like that." Miles encourages **legal** tagging.

But how can tagging not be **illegal**? Some cities like San Francisco have created mural zones where **artists** can **express** themselves without breaking the law. Most people point out that taggers tend to respect each other's work and wouldn't **deface** someone else's piece. In San Diego, a group called Writerz Blok is trying to get **artists** to tag on "**legal** walls."

Can graffiti taggers work within the system? On one side, law enforcement officials say that they have to. On the other side, taggers hold up their spray-paint cans and make a choice.

Fine Arts CONTENT CONNECTION

Artist or Vandal?

Shepard Fairey moves between the halls of power in Washington, DC, and the back alleys of Boston with equal ease. Fairey created the "Hope" poster that was the central image of Barack Obama's 2008 campaign for president.

Three weeks after the presidential portrait was hung in the National Portrait Gallery, police arrested Fairey in Boston. They accused him of illegally posting his work on walls around the city. The police are also cracking down on other famous street artists like Banksy and Twist.

Shepard Fairey became known for his OBEY campaign of stickers, posters, and stencils, such as the posters on the left wall above.

Take a Stand

Is the legal crackdown on graffiti going too far? Would you report any of these people to the police?

1. a recognized artist like Shepard Fairey or Banksy
2. a local writer who does amazing pieces
3. a gang member tagging his territory
4. a tagger who sprays your property

Graffiti on Christina Street

by Ethel Irene Kabwato

Blessing, you and I

Carry memories of the graffiti

On Christina Street,

You and I still carry dreams

Of the day when time stood still

As we marvelled at the walls

And thought of the **political** graffiti

Back home;

Of **politicians** locked in battle

Of youths still struggling

With **identity**- and vote-buying;

Of men and women who

Crossed **borders**

Never to return . . .

But we held onto that dream, Blessing

Of the colourful graffiti

Of new and old arrivants in Cardiff

Chronicling their history on the wall . . .

Of years spent slaving

Somewhere by the seaside

Of pale, grim faces,

Brought to life by paint.

Christina Street does not ring

With children's laughter;

Its quiet strength is in the story

Told through pictures on wall

In cold grey

emptiness;

We watched in awe as pigeons

Paid homage to unknown sojourners

On street walls

As we huddled in our coats . . . to take these memories with us.

They would haunt us

Long after we left . . .

Meet the Author

ETHEL IRENE KABWATO

Born: 1970 in Mutare, Zimbabwe

College: Hillside Teachers College in Bulawayo, Zimbabwe, and Zimbabwe Open University

Projects: Slum Cinema, which builds theaters in slums to show documentaries and trains people to be photographers and videographers. Crossing Borders Project, which connected young African writers with mentors in the United Kingdom.

Family: She and her husband, Lovet Mutisi, have two daughters, Nadia and Wynona.

In Her Own Words: "I write about absence and loss. This is based on personal experiences. Out of about seven siblings, we are the only two who have remained behind in Zimbabwe."

Debate

Should PLASTIC BAGS be free or cost a fee?

Take a look around you. Do you see anything plastic? A water bottle? The bag in the trash can? A ballpoint pen? Well, all that plastic can end up in trash heaps. But many times it ends up in the ocean, where it turns into tiny bits of plastic that end up poisoning our waterways and the animals that live near them.

Some people believe that if we ban plastic bags at stores, we can begin to save the planet. Others think plastic bags aren't the problem. They say the problem is that people use them only once and then throw them away.

Should we ban the bag? How else can we lower the impact plastics have on our planet?

Billions of plastic bags litter our planet. We throw them away . . . but the bags don't go away.

The Problem With Plastic

According to the Environmental Protection Agency, people in the United States use between **70 billion** and **100 billion** plastic bags annually. An average American family takes home **1,500** plastic bags a year, and most of those are not **recycled**. Plastic bags and products contribute to a significant **environmental** problem.

(Environmental Protection Agency, 2014)

- It can take up to **1,000** years for plastic bags to biodegrade, or break down, in landfills.
- **More than a million** birds, marine mammals, and sea turtles die each year as a result of eating or being trapped in plastic.
- Plastic bags make up a large part of the Great Pacific Garbage Patch, a giant mass of trash **polluting** the Pacific Ocean.

(EcoWatch, 2014)

Banned!

The use of plastic bags is the subject of ongoing controversy around the world. Many cities and countries have already banned **disposable** bags.

- Bangladesh banned plastic bags after they **polluted** rivers, clogged drains, and caused flooding that submerged parts of the country.
- A ban in Paris helped France reduce their plastic bag use from **10.5 billion** bags to **1.5 billion** bags in seven years.
- In 2007, San Francisco became the first US city to ban plastic bags. By 2014, **126** US cities and counties passed similar bans.

(Earth Policy Institute, 2014)

Ban It or Bag It?

by Sanjay Malik

Can you imagine a world without plastic bags? Less than 50 years ago, **disposable** plastic bags didn't exist. Now they are everywhere—in stores, homes, locker rooms, and lunchrooms. They float in the air, hang on trees, clog landfills, and **pollute** the oceans.

John Jurinek manages a San Francisco **recycling** plant. He is one of many **environmentalists** on one side of the issue. He believes the government should ban plastic bags. When asked what is wrong with the bags, he answers with one word: "Everything." To him, plastic products cause serious damage to the **environment**. Plastic bags are made from oil products and use up nonrenewable **resources**. They **litter** the air, the land, and—especially—the ocean. Plus, they never completely decompose. They just hang around forever in one toxic form or another.

On the other side of the issue are members of the plastics industry.

They think the bags are just a victim of success. Today, plastic bags account for four out of every five bags handed out at a grocery store. Robert Bateman, a plastic bag manufacturer, explains that **retailers** are giving out too many bags. He argues that **consumers** are not **recycling** them properly. Concerns about the bags "need to be addressed responsibly," he says. However, he does not believe that a ban is the answer.

❶ BAN THE BAGS

Supporters of a ban note other countries, including India

Plastic bags have a disastrous impact on the environment—especially marine life.

and China, that have successfully implemented bans on **disposable** bags. Many US cities also want to find a way to deal with the "urban tumbleweeds" that **litter** their landscapes. San Francisco, California, was the first US city to pass **legislation** to ban plastic bags in 2007. Nashua Kalil works on **environmental** issues with the Zero Waste Commission in nearby Berkeley. "There is an **environmental** cost to these so-called free plastic bags," she says. "Future generations will pay that cost."

"The plastic bags you use will still be around long after you are."

What is that cost? "The plastic bags you use will still be around long after you are," says Stephanie Barger of the Earth **Resource** Foundation, an **environmental** education group. "All the plastic that has been made is still around in smaller and smaller pieces." The bags are also much more than just an eyesore. For wildlife, they can be killers. According to Worldwatch Institute, a pro-**environment** group, tens of thousands of whales, birds, seals, and turtles die from contact with ocean-borne plastic bags. **Supporters** of a ban want to stop a problem that is already overwhelming.

How do opponents of a ban respond? Many think that an outright ban is going too far. Judith McKenney of Silverton, Oregon, says she understands the problem with plastic bags. However, she believes an individual's decision should be based on personal responsibility rather than government **legislation**. "To me, it's a matter of freedom," she adds.

❷ SAVE THE BAGS

Laurie Kusek, a spokesperson for the American Plastics Council, defends the usefulness of plastic bags for **consumers**. "It is important to understand that plastic grocery bags are some of the most **reused** items around the house," she points out. "Many, many bags are **reused** as book and lunch bags as kids head off to school, as trash can liners, and to pick up Fido's droppings off the lawn." Kusek also argues that the plastics industry is encouraging the implementation of **recycling** centers for the bags.

Critics of the ban argue that **consumers** will always need something to put their shopping items in. Banning plastic bags would force people to use paper bags, which create their own **environmental** problems.

According to the American Forest and Paper Association, 14 million trees are cut down to **produce** 10 billion paper grocery bags each year. Also, it takes more energy to **produce** and **recycle** paper bags than plastic bags. In fact, the **production** of paper bags creates more air and water **pollution** than plastic bag **production**.

A Comparison of Bags

Type of Bag	Production and Consumption	Cost to Produce	Cost to Consumer	Reusable or Disposable	Impact on Environment
Paper	Americans use over 10 billion annually, made from about 14 million trees.	5 to 8 cents per bag	free in most cities; 5 cents a bag in some areas	• disposable—15% to 20% get recycled • reusable—for wrapping/packing • biodegradable, or can be broken down	• chemicals used production caus air/water polluti • take up about 1% of space in landfills • landfill gases lea to air pollution
Plastic	The United States consumes 70 to 100 billion yearly, made from about 12 million barrels of oil.	1 to 2 cents per bag	free in most cities; 5 to 25 cents per bag in some areas	• disposable—less than 12% get recycled • reusable—to carry items, line trash cans, and pack • not biodegradable	• chemicals used production caus air pollution • take up 0.4% of space in landfill • can last 1,000 years • kill many animal
Cloth/ Canvas	5% to 10% of the US population uses cloth bags, which are made from polyester, cotton, or other fibers.	10 to 25 cents per bag	99 cents to $15 per bag	• reusable—for 100 or more shopping trips • not biodegradable • must be cleaned to prevent food contamination	• low impact on environment • save energy and resources

How do opponents of plastic bags respond? They point out that less than 12 percent of plastic bags, sacks, and wraps end up being **recycled**. Gordon Bennett of the Sierra Club, America's oldest **environmental** organization, offers this response on the paper versus plastic argument: "The fundamental thing about trees is that if you manage them properly, they're a renewable **resource**. I haven't heard about the oil guys growing any more oil lately."

A ban may not align with most Americans' belief in freedom of choice.

Plastic bags are cheap for retailers, and many consumers find them useful.

❸ NECESSARY ACTION

Ban or no ban, most people agree that something has to **occur** to stop the staggering use of **disposable** plastic bags. Erik Assadourian of the Worldwatch Institute believes that an outright ban can work in countries like India or China, but it may not be **relevant** in the United States. He argues that a ban may not align with most Americans' belief in freedom of choice and **supports** a plastic bag **tax** instead.

Not all **legislators** agree with Assadourian. In 2011, the California Supreme Court voted to uphold the right for cities to ban bags. As of 2014, more than 100 cities have instituted bans, including large cities like Los Angeles and San Francisco.

Some **retail** stores now charge customers for **reusable** bags. **Consumers** may be surprised when this **occurs**, but they accept it. However, the real solution, many people argue, is BYOB— Bring Your Own Bag. Worldwatch Institute states on its website, "the best alternative [to plastic bags] is to carry and **reuse** your own durable cloth bags." For some Americans, that will be a challenge. However, the plastic bag problem is not going away. In fact, it will only get worse.

Can your generation give up plastic bags? The future of the planet is yours to decide.

Social Studies CONTENT CONNECTION

The Great Pacific Garbage Patch

The Great Pacific Garbage Patch is a floating mass of garbage in the Pacific Ocean.

Location: midway between Hawaii and California

Contents: tons of litter, such as wrappers, plastic bags, toys, pacifiers, and toothbrushes—about 90% is plastic products

Size: estimated at twice the size of Texas and 90 feet deep

Formation: The Great Pacific Garbage Patch is an ocean gyre, a system of rotating ocean currents. The Pacific Gyre pulls trash from the coasts of North America and Japan.

Take a Stand

Who should be responsible for cleaning up the Great Pacific Garbage Patch?
1. governments of countries that border the Pacific Ocean
2. large corporations that manufacture plastic products
3. shipping companies that dump waste into the ocean
4. nonprofit organizations that advocate for the environment

With Millions of Tons of Plastic in Oceans, More Scientists Studying Impact

by Laura Parker

The amount of global trash is expected to rise every year for the rest of the century. With no intervention, the growing garbage heap won't even peak by 2021. Since most marine debris originates on land, that grim prognosis could spell disaster for the oceans. It's creating an **environmental** hazard often compared in scope with climate change.

"We estimate we're going to have millions of tons of plastic going into the ocean with, so far, unknown consequences," says Jenna Jambeck, an **environmental** engineer. She is among a group of scientists pursuing a new phase of research on ocean trash and measuring its impact on the **environment** and marine life.

The dilemma caused by the growing tonnage of mostly plastic debris is so complex, it has created a new interdisciplinary field of study. Scientists like Jambeck are examining many new issues that range from the toxicity of plastics ingested by marine animals to the politics and economics of solid waste management in developing nations.

> **"We estimate we're going to have millions of tons of plastic going into the ocean with, so far, unknown consequences."**

NEW QUESTIONS FOR AN OLD PROBLEM

Seafarers have known for decades that the oceans are trash dumps. They are the ultimate sinkholes for

Beach cleanups reduce pollution, but are costly and ineffective.

after Congress passed the Marine Debris Act at the urging of Senator Daniel Inouye.

The defining moment of ocean debris research, says Jambeck, was when scientists discovered that ocean debris was no longer made of cloth, wood, and ceramics. Instead it was composed almost entirely of plastic. Most of that is microplastic that has decayed and broken down into microscopic pieces that float in the water column.

"Once microplastics entered the picture and it was being ingested by marine life, it was a whole new ballgame," Jambeck says. "That's when the alarms started going off."

all global garbage. So far, 136 species of marine animals have been found entangled in debris. According to the National Oceanic and Atmospheric Administration (NOAA), the first such discovery was made in 1944. Then, northern fur seals turned up trapped in rubber "collars" that were the remains of Japanese food-drop bags from World War II.

But scientific research into marine garbage is only a decade or so old. The NOAA, for example, launched its Marine Debris Program only in 2006,

Jambeck and her team's research will provide new estimates of how much garbage is **produced** globally every year. It will show how much garbage comes from developing countries lacking garbage collection systems. And it will determine how much **litter** is **produced** by developed countries. All trash has the **potential** to reach the oceans.

Despite the new burst of scientific study, solving the problem in the face of an increasing volume of ocean trash seems an almost insurmountable task.

OPTIONS ARE FEW: CLEANUP OR PREVENTION

An alliance of 48 plastic manufacturers from 25 countries has pledged to help prevent marine debris and encourage **recycling**. Several manufacturers are now marketing products made partly from **recycled** ocean plastics and abandoned fishing gear.

Floating debris is constantly moving, shifting with the seasonal weather, and changing in shape and size.

But the consensus among many scientists is that cleaning up the oceans can **potentially** cause more harm than good. Cleaning up microplastics could also inadvertently sweep up plankton. These organisms provide the basis for the marine food chain and half of the photosynthesis on Earth.

Ocean trash is driven by currents into loosely formed garbage "patches" that Dianna Parker, a NOAA spokesperson, says are more

Ocean garbage patches are like a "peppery soup" of tiny plastic bits.

accurately described as "peppery soup." They are filled with grain-size plastic bits. The word *patch* suggests a defined size and location. But in fact floating debris is constantly moving, shifting with the seasonal weather, and changing in shape and size.

Cleaning up even one of these areas seems impossible. Not surprisingly, the largest patch is in the largest ocean, the Pacific, which covers a third of the planet. The Great Pacific Garbage Patch is often said to be twice the size of Texas. It actually extends, at times, from Japan to San Francisco. It also varies in shape and density. According to the NOAA, cleaning up less than one percent of the North Pacific would take 68 ships working 10 hours a day for a year.

Beach cleanups help, but are costly and **ineffective**. The Ocean Conservancy, the international leader in coastal cleanups, has collected some 180 million tons in three decades of work. "We have now created the world's best database for what actually happens on our beaches," says Andreas Merkl, the group's CEO.

According to the NOAA, cleaning up less than one percent of the North Pacific would take 68 ships working 10 hours a day for a year.

But as long as some countries lack the ability to efficiently collect garbage from its citizens, that garbage will continue to end up in the ocean.

Most ocean trash used to be cloth, wood, and ceramics. Now, it is almost all plastic.

Bye-Bye Bags and Bottles: This Woman Lives Plastic Free

by Kristine Wong

A baby albatross with a stomach full of plastic trash changed Beth Terry's life.

The Oakland, California–based accountant had been living on a diet of frozen dinners and plastic-wrapped energy bars her entire adult life. She'd regularly buy beverages in plastic bottles without a second thought.

But in the summer of 2007, she heard a radio interview with Colin Beavan. Beavan, over the course of 12 months, deliberately **generated** as little garbage as possible. That day she visited Beavan's blog to learn about his No Impact Project, which promotes living a "zero-waste lifestyle." On it she saw the photograph of the dead albatross. Its parents had likely fed it the plastic, thinking that it was food. "Seeing that photo shocked me into action," says Terry. "The baby was full of plastic stuff that I used every day."

Since then, Terry reduced her annual plastic waste to 2 percent of the national average. She launched a blog, *My Plastic-Free Life*. And she wrote a book, *Plastic Free: How I Kicked the Plastic Habit and How You Can Too*.

Beth Terry tries to lead a plastic-free lifestyle. She uses 98% less plastic than the average American.

Terry began her conversion to a virtually plastic-free lifestyle gradually, knowing this would make it easier to succeed. First she used up an item she already had at home. Then she tried to find a plastic-free version. "I would ask myself if I could live without it. And if not, then I would keep using it until I could find an **alternative**," she said.

She also wanted to know her personal plastic footprint. So each week she collected her plastic waste, tallied it, and posted a photo along with the results on her blog.

By 2009, she had generated 3.7 pounds of plastic for the entire year. That's about 4 percent of the US per capita average.

The first week Terry tracked her usage, her plastic waste weighed 20 ounces. And her footprint kept shrinking. By 2009, she had **generated** 3.7 pounds of plastic for the entire year. That's about 4 percent of the US per capita average.

To this day—with the help of a lot of glass jars and **reusable** cloth sacks—Terry uses a minimal amount of plastic. She still uses prescription bottles (which cannot be **reused**) and the small plastic rings that are sealed around glass jars.

Terry maintains her almost plastic-free life by adhering to the following eight guidelines:

1. Use glass jars and stainless steel containers of all sizes to store your food. They can also be used to package your lunch.

2. Avoid the plastic tubs that hold berries by buying fruit at the farmers' market. You can put the fruit in your own reusable bag. Then give the containers back to the farmer on the spot or return them the next time you go.

3. Bring **reusable** sacks and containers to the grocery store or farmers' market. (Terry puts bread in the sacks and fish and cheese in the containers.)

4. Find markets that sell locally **produced** milk and yogurt in ceramic or glass containers and

Beth Terry suggests bringing reusable containers and sacks when grocery shopping.

return them empty to the store for **reuse**.

5. Bring your own doggie bag (**reusable** container) to restaurants.

6. Carry around a set of your own **reusable** utensils.

7. Consider making your own household cleaners, deodorant, shampoo, and conditioner to cut down on plastic-bottle consumption. (Terry makes her own deodorant using baking soda and tea tree oil. She also uses the "no shampoo" method of washing and conditioning her hair with baking soda and apple cider vinegar.)

8. Wear as little synthetic clothing as possible. (Terry says that the one synthetic-free item she hasn't been able to find is underwear. She invites anyone who makes a synthetic-free version to contact her.)

Terry realizes that some things just can't be found without plastic packaging. In instances like these, she recommends buying the largest size available. Then you can portion it into smaller sizes at home.

"At this point, it's really easy for me to live this way, but it wasn't always that way," she said. "The hardest part is doing research and finding the **alternatives**."

Debate

Could text talk actually be better than real talk?

Teens send more text messages than any other age group. Some experts say that all this texting changes how we write, talk to others, and deal with problems—and not always in a good way.

But what do you think? Does texting hurt the way young people talk and write, or can texting make writing, talking, and getting help with troubling issues easier?

Let's look at how texting influences what young people do IRL (in real life)!

Data File

Texting among teens has been on the rise for the last decade. Is it ruining the way we talk and write, or making us better at it?

To Text or Talk?

Texting has become the leading way teens "talk" to each other.

- Teens send an average of 60 texts per day.
- 63% of teens say that they send and receive texts every day, while only 39% of teens talk daily on their cell phones. 35% speak face-to-face to classmates outside of school each day.

(Pew Research Center, 2012)

Texting for Good

Many organizations and young people are using texting as a force for change.

- In 2007, the Mobile Giving Foundation launched, giving cell phone users the opportunity to text donations to charities *(Mobile Giving Foundation, 2014)*.
- In 2010, 19% of people ages 18–29 gave money to charities using text donations. 26% of the same age range mailed their donations to charities *(Nieman Journalism Lab, 2010)*.
- As of March 2015, the Crisis Text Line has exchanged more than 5.5 million texts with teens seeking help with issues like bullying, depression, and abuse *(Crisis Text Line, 2015)*.
- In 2014, the Federal Communications Commission ruled that cell phone service providers must allow customers to text emergencies to local 911 services *(Federal Communications Commission, 2014)*.

luv 2 txt

Some adults may not believe this, but it turns out that texting helps teens be healthy and happy.

by Natalie Smith

1 Text messaging is Callie Owens's favorite way to **communicate**. The 17-year-old from Waynesboro, Virginia, sends 100 to 200 texts each day. She texts while she's hanging out with her friends, when she's working on her homework, and even during class!

Callie isn't alone. A recent survey by the Pew Internet and American Life project found that one-third of US cell-phone users ages 12 to 17 send more than 100 texts daily. But not everyone is a fan of this **constant** stream of **communication**.

"My parents tell me that I text too much," Callie says. "When I'm doing my homework, they'll ask, 'Isn't that **distracting** you?'"

Experts say texting can benefit teens and help them make strong connections.

Sound familiar? With texting on the rise, many parents worry that all the jabbering via keyboards is harmful to kids. But some experts say texting can actually benefit teens! "I think, from everything we've seen, it's a good thing that they have more **connections**," says Larry Rosen, a psychology professor at California State University.

Rosen studies how teens and families use and react to different types of **technology**.

> **"It's fast communication. I think it's easier than calling because you can still be doing something else while texting. You don't have to give your undivided attention to it."**

❷ Texting Benefits

Rosen **admits constant** texting can be unhealthy in some situations. But when texting is used **constructively**, experts say it can improve teens' social, language, and **technical** skills.

Texting—or sending short messages from one cell phone to another—first became available with major US cell-phone providers in the early 2000s. Its popularity has grown rapidly, with teens texting more than any other age group. Texting is their primary medium for interacting with friends, according to the Pew survey.

"It's fast **communication**," says Jenny Kreps, 15, of Ridgefield, Connecticut. "I think it's easier than calling because you can still be doing something else while texting. You don't have to give your undivided attention to it."

But is all this texting turning teens into antisocial phone addicts? Scott Campbell, assistant professor of **communication** studies at the University of Michigan, has studied the role of cell phones in teens' lives and was a coauthor of the Pew survey. Campbell believes that texting is actually strengthening teens' social **bonds**.

❸ Building Bonds

"They're using the **technology** to **connect** with their peers and be sociable, which is important for them at that point in life," Campbell says. "They're figuring out who they are and what they're about. The way they do that is through **connections** with other people."

Texting helps Matt Schlegel, 16, of Camp Hill, Pennsylvania, manage his social life. "I made a lot of friends when I was in my school musical," he says. "But I don't have classes with them because they're in different grades, so I'll text them to see how they're doing."

Some educators fear that texting encourages **improper** punctuation and sentence structure, which may negatively **affect** students' writing skills. Many researchers, though, disagree.

Rosen and his colleagues at California State University recently studied the relationship between "textisms" and **formal**

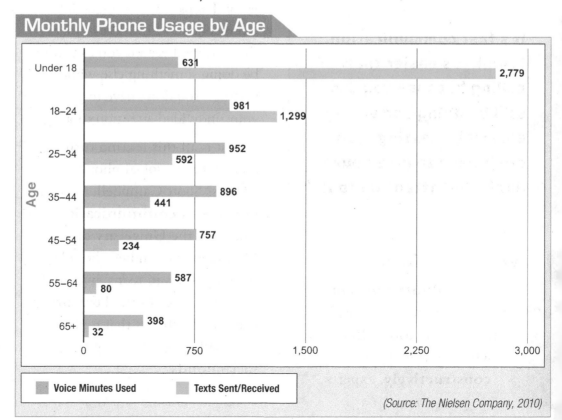

Monthly Phone Usage by Age

Age	Voice Minutes Used	Texts Sent/Received
Under 18	631	2,779
18–24	981	1,299
25–34	952	592
35–44	896	441
45–54	757	234
55–64	587	80
65+	398	32

(Source: The Nielsen Company, 2010)

In Texting Era, Crisis Hotlines Put Help at Youths' Fingertips

by Leslie Kaufman

The conversation began abruptly, with the anonymous teenager getting straight to the point: She had just told her family that she was really a boy trapped in a female body. "Now my family hates me," she told a **crisis counselor**.

The **counselor** was empathetic. She asked for more detail about the family, offered encouragement, and provided the name of a local support group.

It was in many ways a typical exchange on a **crisis** hotline, except it took place entirely by texting.

While **counseling** by phone remains far more prevalent, texting has become such a fundamental way to **communicate**, particularly

Text counseling can give teens a private way to seek support.

among people under 20. **Crisis** groups have begun to adopt it as an alternative way of providing emergency services and **counseling**.

> **While counseling by phone remains far more prevalent, texting has become such a fundamental way to communicate, particularly among people under 20.**

Texting provides privacy that can be crucial if a person feels threatened by someone near him or her, **counselors** say. It also looks more natural if the teenager is in public. "They can still look 'cool' to their peers or friends while receiving assistance that they are in desperate need of," said Jerry Weichman. Weichman is a clinical psychologist in Newport Beach, California, who deals with adolescent issues.

The adoption of texting extends beyond just **crisis** groups. By May 2014, the four largest phone companies had promised to make it **technologically** possible to text 911 anywhere in the country.

It is also possible to reach broader organizations like the National Dating Abuse Helpline by text.

Crisis Text Line, a nonprofit based in New York, started offering text **counseling** in August of 2013, delivering services through partnerships with six separate hotlines across the country. Since then, the group says, it has exchanged nearly one million texts with 19,000 teenagers.

Dr. Weichman, the psychologist, said that with texting, teenagers could keep their conversations and can review them at a later date. Nancy Lublin, the founder of the Crisis Text Line, said her group had received messages from distressed teenagers who were in the same room with their abusers, who might not have reached out by phone.

Often, Ms. Lublin said, Crisis Text Line's job is to help the texter find support close to home.

Ms. Lublin said texts also provided real-time information that showed patterns for people in **crisis**.

This spring, Crisis Text Line intends to make the data available to the public. "My dream," Ms. Lublin said, "is that public health officials will use this data and tailor public policy solutions around it."

The idea for Crisis Text Line began two years ago when the main nonprofit organization run by Ms. Lublin, DoSomething.org, which encourages teenagers to get involved in causes like animal cruelty, received a chilling text about abuse.

Although DoSomething regularly **communicates** with its members by text, it had no **crisis** capabilities. Legally, DoSomething was allowed to text back a hotline phone number, but no more. It never heard back.

Crisis Text Line founder Nancy Lublin hopes the data she collects from text counseling sessions will help change how teens receive care.

After spending weeks sleepless with worry, Ms. Lublin decided that if teenagers were in a threatening situation and wanted to text with a **counselor** instead of talk, there should be a way. She started fund-raising and hired a team of programmers who toured hotline centers.

People texting for help receive the same services as those calling in. But the interaction plays out much differently, **crisis** experts say.

> **After spending weeks sleepless with worry, Ms. Lublin decided that if teenagers were in a threatening situation and wanted to text with a counselor instead of talk, there should be a way.**

Texters tend to be more immediately in **crisis** than callers, the **crisis** experts say. Phones attract the lonely and pranksters the way text does not.

Ron White, chief program officer for Samaritans Inc., a suicide prevention organization in Boston that is part of the Crisis Text Line network, started using its texting service in August of 2013. He says that texting conversations will have more pauses and play out over a longer time. But for some reason texting conversations tend to be much more direct.

"On the phone there is some time building a rapport," he said, "but young people on text tend to get right to the point. They go from zero to 60 in a couple of seconds."

Beata Momtaz, who has worked both the phone and text hotlines for Samaritan, says that she prefers texting because she thinks it is the way teenagers most like to **communicate**. Still, she said, there are challenges.

"On the phone you have the ability to moderate what you are saying with your tone," she said. "With text for me when I started doing it, I had to think about my words and how to say something a little more softly."

Also, she said, resolution can be more confusing. "With text they can disappear a lot more easily than the phone," Ms. Momtaz said. "People rarely end a phone call by randomly hanging up."

That said, with texting, a conversation is never really over, she said. The minute the texter writes back, whether it is an hour later or a week later, the system will automatically pull up the previous messages for the **counselor** on duty. Then they can begin again.

Social Studies

CONTENT CONNECTION

Texting for Safety

In 2014, the Federal Communications Commission announced that cell phone companies must allow customers to contact 911 by text. Text-to-911 could help those in too much danger to make a phone call. But some people wonder about its effectiveness:

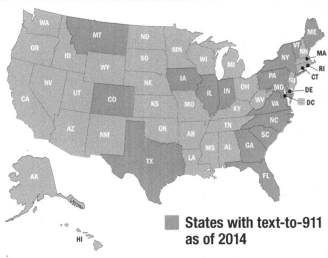

■ **States with text-to-911 as of 2014**

(Source: Federal Communications Commission, 2014)

- 911 centers have a hard time getting accurate locations from texters.
- As of August 2014, only two percent of 911 emergency centers in the country were prepared to take text messages.
- Lawmakers argue that forcing text messaging software to have location information could lead to privacy issues.

However, within months of the ruling, 12 states started using text-to-911. It looks like emergency texting is here to stay.

Take a Stand

Do you think emergency texting services will be useful for people who need help fast? Why or why not?

Debate What makes someone a
GOOD FRIEND?

A good friend can be tough to find. Researchers say we can expect to have an average of 150 friends in our lifetimes. But which of those friends will mean the most to us? What, exactly, makes our closest friends so dear?

Is it a sense of humor? Or could a close friend be someone who shares your deepest interests, or someone who's your opposite? For some, a close friendship might mean finding someone you can *just be yourself* around.

When it comes to friends, what makes someone move from your "buddy" to your "bestie"?

Bridge to Terabithia: A Play With Music

by Katherine Paterson and Stephanie S. Tolan

CHARACTERS

JESSE AARONS—age 10, Virginia farm boy who draws and runs

LESLIE BURKE—age 10, newly arrived from Arlington, a lover of reading and fantasy

MAY BELLE AARONS—Jesse's six-year-old sister

JANICE AVERY—13-year-old school bully, large, unlovely, and slow

MISS EDMUNDS—young, pretty, liberal, and caring, she teaches fifth grade and music at Lark Creek Elementary

GARY FULCHER—supposedly the fastest runner in the fifth grade

GIRL—5th grader

*Names in **bold** are major roles.*

---

❶ ACT I, Scene 4

LIGHTS UP on school area, MISS EDMUNDS on stool, tuning guitar. JESSE enters, holding papers almost behind his back.

MISS EDMUNDS. Come on in, Jess— no, it's fine. I'm just getting ready for music class. How was your summer?

JESSE. Okay, I guess.

MISS EDMUNDS. Did you get time to do any more drawings?

JESSE. Yes'm. Some.

MISS EDMUNDS. Well? Did you bring them? *(HE nods.)* Let me see. You know how much I like your drawings. Remember that hippopotamus you did last year? The one falling over the cliff? *(HE nods.)* What was it saying?

JESSE. "I seem to have forgot my glasses."

MISS EDMUNDS. *(Laughing.)* That's it! I'll never forget the **expression** on that animal's face. Perfect. *(SHE holds out her hand to him.)* Let's see the new ones.

> # They just don't appreciate your talent yet, Jess.

(HE hesitates.)

MISS EDMUNDS. Jesse Aarons, hand them over!

(HE does. SHE looks at them, nodding, making comments— "nice," "funny," "that's good," etc. Takes longer at one, looks at others, then back to the one.)

MISS EDMUNDS. I like them, Jess. All of them. But especially this one.

JESSE. You can keep it, if you want.

MISS EDMUNDS. Well, thanks! Why don't I hang it up so everybody can **admire** it?

JESSE. *(Uncomfortable.)* I just did it to show you. The guys'll make fun of it.

MISS EDMUNDS. They just don't appreciate your talent yet, Jess. Meantime, I'll hang this up at home. All right?

JESSE. *(It's more than all right.)* Yes'm.

*(BELL rings and other KIDS come in, chattering about the race. MISS EDMUNDS puts the drawing beneath her stool and greets them as they enter. JESSE puts his drawings into his desk and gazes **adoringly** at Miss Edmunds. LESLIE comes in, tries to speak to Jess. HE turns away. SHE sits.)*

MISS EDMUNDS. *(To Leslie.)* How's your first day going, Leslie?

GARY. You gotta talk to her, Miss Edmunds. She don't understand about recess.

GIRL. Oh, Gary's just mad because she beat him.

GARY. *(Hotly.)* She don't know how to act at this school.

(KIDS snicker.)

JANICE. Or how to dress! *(SHE has opened her purse and is elaborately applying hand lotion.)*

(Guffaws from CLASS.)

MISS EDMUNDS. *(Interrupting.)* This year, class, we'll have music on Tuesday afternoons.

I think it'll be more fun if we just push back the desks and you can sit in a circle on the floor.

JANICE. But I just got a new dress!

MISS EDMUNDS. Well, that's fine Janice—you just sit there in your seat. Anyone else who is worried about their clothes today—

(There is confusion for a moment as GIRLS decide what to do, while BOYS cluster around Miss Edmunds on the floor. GIRLS stay in their seats, except for LESLIE, who joins the boys. SHE sits close to Jess. HE moves away.)

MISS EDMUNDS. Do you like to sing, Leslie?

LESLIE. Yes.

MISS EDMUNDS. Perhaps you'd like to choose a song for us to begin with.

JANICE. How about "I Got Plenty A Nothin'?"

(KIDS except JESS laugh. LESLIE pretends not to notice.)

MISS EDMUNDS. Maybe what we should do is learn a new song. I think I have just the thing. Listen, now. Carefully! *(Begins singing.)*

[Music Cue #5: DIFFERENCES]

IF EVERY FLOWER
WERE A ROSE

AND EVERY ROSE WAS RED

IF EVERY SKY WERE
CLOUDLESS BLUE

AND ALL OUR FOOD
WAS BREAD—

THERE'D BE NO
DIFFERENCE.

WHAT ARE THE
DIFFERENCES FOR?

WITHOUT A DIFFERENCE
THE WORLD WOULD
BE A BORE.

(Speaks.)

That's the **chorus**. Try it with me.

> What are the
> differences for?
> Without a difference
> The world would
> be a bore.

ALL. *(Sing, KIDS experimentally.)*

THERE'D BE NO
DIFFERENCE.

WHAT ARE THE
DIFFERENCES FOR?

WITHOUT A DIFFERENCE

THE WORLD WOULD
BE A BORE.

*(As they sing, JESS and
LESLIE look at each other,
appreciating the lyrics. LESLIE
smiles. JESS smiles back.)*

MISS EDMUNDS. Okay, I'll do
the verses now, and you join
me when I get to the **chorus**.

IF EVERY PERSON
WERE A KID

AND EVERY KID
WAS WHITE

IF EVERY FINGER
WERE A THUMB

AND BOTH OUR HANDS
WERE RIGHT—

ALL. *(Singing.)*

THERE'D BE NO
DIFFERENCE.

WHAT ARE THE
DIFFERENCES FOR?

WITHOUT A DIFFERENCE

THE WORLD WOULD
BE A BORE.

MISS EDMUNDS. *(Singing.)*

IF EVERY SONG HAD
JUST ONE NOTE

AND EVERY NOTE WAS C

IF EVERY BOOK HAD
JUST ONE WORD

AND EVERY WORD
WAS "ME"—

ALL. *(Singing.)*

THERE'D BE NO
DIFFERENCE.

WHAT ARE THE
DIFFERENCES FOR?

WITHOUT A DIFFERENCE

THE WORLD WOULD
BE A BORE.

*(By the time the song is over
LESLIE has moved closer to
JESS and he hasn't moved away.
THEY are both enjoying both
the song and the singing.)*

MISS EDMUNDS. All right, class,
that was good. Let me go back
and we'll try it again. *(SHE
begins to repeat the last verse softly.)*

LESLIE. *(In a loud whisper to
Jess.)* She's really nice.

JESSE. *(**Emphatically**.)* Yeah.

LESLIE. One nice thing
about this school.

JESSE. I guess you hate it here.

LESLIE. Yeah.

*(BOTH join **chorus** and
finish song with others.)*

MISS EDMUNDS. One more time—

ALL. *(Singing.)*

THERE'D BE NO DIFFERENCE.

WHAT ARE THE DIFFERENCES FOR?

WITHOUT A DIFFERENCE THE WORLD WOULD BE A BORE.

[Music Cue #5A: DIFFERENCES Underscore]

BLACKOUT

❷ *LIGHTS UP on JESS and LESLIE walking from left, MAY BELLE running, skipping to keep up. Fence set piece now has sign that reads, "FREE PUPPIES." MAY BELLE stops to try to sound it out—JESS and LESLIE go a little ahead, not noticing her.*

JESSE. I'll bet your other school was lots bigger.

LESLIE. It sure was. It even had a gym.

JESSE. A whole, separate room?

LESLIE. Sure. We had gymnastics, too. I was good at that.

JESSE. *(Almost to himself.)* Like running.

LESLIE. Running's fun, too. Hey, I was trying to tell you before—thanks for taking my side about the race.

MAY BELLE. Jesse! What's a fuh-ree puh-mm-pp-pyes?

> # It wasn't nothin'. Gary Fulcher thinks he's everybody's boss.

JESSE. *(Ignoring May Belle.)* It wasn't nothin'. Gary Fulcher thinks he's everybody's boss.

LESLIE. Well, he sure isn't the fastest runner.

MAY BELLE. Jesse!

JESSE. No, I guess he ain't.

MAY BELLE. Jesse Aarons, I'm talkin' to you!

JESSE. Why'd you move to Lark Creek?

LESLIE. Bill and Judy wanted to **reassess** their **priorities**.

MAY BELLE. Who's Bill and Judy?

LESLIE. My parents.

MAY BELLE. Huh?

LESLIE. They wanted to get away from the city and decide what's really important to them.

JESSE. Don't they care what's important to you?

LESLIE. I wanted to come, too. You never know ahead of time what something's really going to be like.

> Yeah. Well. Difference between you and me is everyone thinks you're weird. Me— I *am* weird.

MAY BELLE. Don't you like Lark Creek, Leslie? I do. I like first grade lots. I like everything. Except Janice Avery. She's mean to first graders.

JESSE. She's mean to everybody, May Belle.

MAY BELLE. She scares me.

LESLIE. Don't let her. She's nothing but a dumb cow—

MAY BELLE. My cow is not dumb, is she, Jess?

JESSE. Well, Miss Bessie is kinda in a class by herself. She ain't like most cows.

LESLIE. *(Singing a capella.)*

THERE'D BE NO DIFFERENCE.

WHAT ARE DIFFERENCES FOR?

JESSE. *(Laughing.)* You like that song?

LESLIE. Didn't you? Do you think she—? I mean, I felt as though Miss Edmunds knew I was feeling weird and so she chose it especially to make me feel better.

JESSE. Oh.

LESLIE. What? You didn't think so?

JESSE. I thought—I reckon I thought she chose it for me.

LESLIE. But you—

JESSE. *(Grinning.)* Yeah. Well. Difference between you and me is everyone thinks you're weird. Me—I *am* weird.

LESLIE. You're not weird.

JESSE. I don't know. I'm always drawing.

LESLIE. What's wrong with drawing?

MAY BELLE. I draw! I can draw!

LESLIE. Come on, Jess, Picasso wasn't a sissy. Or Rembrandt.

JESSE. Who?

MAY BELLE. *(No one is paying attention to her.)* Jessee!

LESLIE. *(To Jess.)* Hey, do you think we could do something this afternoon?

JESSE. I don't know—

MAY BELLE. Me, too! I wanna do something, too.

JESSE. Nobody's asking you, May Belle.

LESLIE. It's not that we don't want you, May Belle. It's just that we've got something special to do—

JESSE. Yeah, May Belle. This is just something for me and Leslie. Why don't you carry my books home and tell Momma I'm over at the neighbors' so she won't worry, okay?

MAY BELLE. You're always tryin' to treat me like a baby. *(SHE sits down.)* I'm going to sit right here in this road and I ain't moving till you let me play with you.

LESLIE. May Belle, how would you like a box of crayons?

MAY BELLE. Has it got red?

LESLIE. Two different kinds of red.

JESSE. Wow!

MAY BELLE. What's the matter with 'em?

LESLIE. I just don't use crayons much anymore. Why don't you take them home and try them out?

MAY BELLE. Well . . .

> You're always tryin' to treat me like a baby. I'm going to sit right here in this road and I ain't moving till you let me play with you.

JESSE. Go on, May Belle. And if you want, you can have a piece of my notebook paper to draw on.

MAY BELLE. Three pieces.

JESSE. Two.

MAY BELLE. Meany! *(But SHE takes crayons and runs off.)*

(LESLIE and JESS look at each other.)

LESLIE. What do you want to do?

JESSE. I don't know. What do you want to do?

LESLIE. *(Laughs.)* What do you usually do after school?

JESSE. Milk the cow.

LESLIE. Oh, that's great. You could teach me how.

JESSE. I don't do it for fun. C'mon. I'll show you something.

(THEY walk toward UC platform as LIGHT COMES UP on rope. JESS grabs it and begins to swing.)

LESLIE. I think that's great about the song.

JESSE. What about it?

LESLIE. The way both of us thought Miss Edmunds had chosen it for us.

JESSE. Yeah. I didn't think you cared what those creeps thought.

LESLIE. I don't. We don't need them do we?

JESSE. Nah—bunch of animals—

LESLIE. Don't **insult** the animal **kingdom**!

JESSE. You called Janice a cow.

LESLIE. My apologies to the cow. *(Bows toward pasture.)* And to monkeys and wolves and skunks and sharks and all the animals we **insult** by comparing them with people.

JESSE. Sharks? Why would you apologize to sharks? They kill people.

LESLIE. Sure, but only to eat. We kill them for sport. Wolves and eagles and killer whales are almost extinct. We just kill and kill and kill. Animals have got just as much right to live as we do! **Predators** too!

JESSE. Okay, okay. I promise not to kill another whale as long as I live.

LESLIE. *(Laughing.)* I'll hold you to that, you human, you!

❸ *(SHE watches JESS swing for a moment.)*

LESLIE. Say—do you know what we need?

JESSE. What?

[Music cue #6: Underscore to TERABITHIA]

LESLIE. We need a place just for us. *(Pauses a moment, thinking.)*

JESSE. Like a fort?

LESLIE. No, not a fort, more like a castle—a castle **stronghold** with turrets and towers and parapets—

JESSE. With what?

LESLIE. It would be so secret that we would never tell anyone in the whole world about it. *(Almost in a whisper.)* It might be a whole secret country—

JESSE. A secret country? That sounds good.

LESLIE. And you and I could be the **rulers** of it.

JESSE. Yeah. You mean like King and Queen—

LESLIE. Right. You know, like Narnia. You've read those books—

(JESS shakes his head.)

LESLIE. Well, like *The Book of Three* and *The Magic Cauldron*.

(HE shakes his head.)

LESLIE. You haven't read those either?

(HE shakes his head again, embarrassed.)

LESLIE. It's okay. I'll lend them to you. You do know about magic **kingdoms**, don't you?

JESSE. I saw Disney World on TV.

LESLIE. In magic **kingdoms** the animals can speak.

JESSE. Like Mickey Mouse.

LESLIE. Well, in a way. And

there are fairy folk and nymphs and dryads and fauns—

JESSE. I know about fawns. They're baby deer.

> Our kingdom will be a wonderful place, you'll see. We just have to figure out where to build the castle stronghold.

LESLIE. This kind of faun is different. He has legs like a goat and a body like a man, with horns and little pointed ears.

JESSE. Weird.

LESLIE. No, you'll like them. Our **kingdom** will be a wonderful place, you'll see. We just have to figure out where to build the castle **stronghold**.

(JESS looks around uncertainly.)

LESLIE. There—across this gully.

JESSE. That's the creek.

Leslie. Creek? Where's the water?

Jesse. Well, it's dried up now.

Leslie. Creek, huh? A magic secret country with a creek? I don't like the sound of that. Let's call it a river. And we'll have our place over there—I know! It could have a magic entrance like Narnia. The only way you can get in is by swinging across on this **enchanted** rope. (*Takes rope from him and runs and swings across.*) Come on!

(*JESS swings across. LESLIE looks around critically.*)

Leslie. This might be a good place. How about right here?

Jesse. Sure. It's almost flat. This'd be a good place to build.

Leslie. (*Picks up a stick, takes a tissue out of her pocket and puts it on top.*) I claim you and name you—Tera . . . Terabithia.

Jesse. Tera—?

Leslie. Terabithia. And we are the **rulers**.

Jesse. I'm the King.

Leslie. Yes. You're the King. And I'm the Queen.

Meet the Author

KATHERINE PATERSON

Born: 1932 in Huai'n, China

Books: Paterson is the author of many award-winning novels (*Jacob Have I Loved*, *The Great Gilly Hopkins*). *The Bridge to Terabithia* was the first of Katherine Paterson's books to be adapted into a movie. The 2007 version stars Josh Hutcherson as Jesse and AnnaSophia Robb as Leslie.

In Her Own Words: "*Bridge to Terabithia* is loosely based on my son's friendship and the death of his friend. But the resemblance stops there, because [Leslie and Jesse] are different people. Their families are different. They live in a different place. So it is fiction and not fact, but it grew out of a real incident."

Our Good Day

by Sandra Cisneros

If you give me five dollars I will be your friend forever. That's what the little one tells me.

Five dollars is cheap since I don't have any friends except Cathy who is only my friend till Tuesday.

Five dollars, five dollars.

She is trying to get somebody to chip in so they can buy a bicycle from this kid named Tito. They already have ten dollars and all they need is five more.

Only five dollars, she says.

Don't talk to them, says Cathy. Can't you see they smell like a broom.

But I like them. Their clothes are crooked and old. They are wearing shiny Sunday shoes without socks. It makes their bald ankles all red, but I like them. Especially the big one who laughs with all her teeth. I like her even though she lets the little one do all the talking.

Five dollars, the little one says, only five.

Cathy is tugging my arm and I know whatever I do next will make her mad forever.

> I wish my name was Cassandra or Alexis or Maritza—anything but Esperanza—but when I tell them my name they don't laugh.

Wait a minute, I say, and run inside to get the five dollars. I have three dollars saved and I take two of Nenny's. She's not home, but I'm sure she'll be glad when she finds out we own a bike. When I get back, Cathy is gone like I knew she would be, but I don't care. I have two new friends and a bike too.

My name is Lucy, the big one says. This here is Rachel my sister.

I'm her sister, says Rachel. Who are you?

Neighbors Lucy and Rachel befriend Esperanza in a play based on *The House on Mango Street*.

And I wish my name was Cassandra or Alexis or Maritza—anything but Esperanza—but when I tell them my name they don't laugh.

We come from Texas, Lucy says and grins. Her was born here, but I'm Texas.

You mean *she*, I say.

No, I'm from Texas, and doesn't get it.

This bike is three ways ours, says Rachel who is thinking ahead already. Mine today, Lucy's tomorrow, and yours day after.

But everybody wants to ride it today because the bike is new, so we decide to take turns *after* tomorrow. Today it belongs to all of us.

I don't tell them about Nenny just yet. It's too **complicated**. Especially since Rachel almost put out Lucy's eye about who was going to get to ride it first. But finally we agree to ride it together. Why not?

Because Lucy has long legs she pedals. I sit on the back seat and Rachel is skinny enough to get up on the handlebars which makes the bike all wobbly as if the wheels are spaghetti, but after a bit you get used to it.

We ride fast and faster. Past my house, sad and red and crumbly in places, past Mr. Benny's grocery on the corner, and down the avenue which is dangerous. Laundromat, junk store, drugstore, windows and cars and more cars, and around the block back to Mango.

People on the bus wave. A very fat lady crossing the street says, You sure got quite a load there.

Rachel shouts, You got quite a load there too. She is very sassy.

> But everybody wants to ride it today because the bike is new, so we decide to take turns after tomorrow. Today it belongs to all of us.

Down, down Mango Street we go. Rachel, Lucy, me. Our new bicycle. Laughing down the crooked ride back.

Meet the Author

SANDRA CISNEROS

Born: 1954 in Chicago, Illinois

Books: Many books of fiction and poetry for children and adults, including *My Wicked Wicked Ways*, *Woman Hollering Creek and Other Stories*, *Hairs/Pelitos*, *Caramelo*, and *The House on Mango Street*.

In Her Own Words: "[*The House on Mango Street* is] a young girl's diary in a sense. All the stories are told from the point of view of a woman-girl who is . . . between childhood and adulthood. Some days she's a child and for a few days she might be an adult. That always struck me as a kind of mysterious time, so I chose her as the persona for these stories."

Where Is She Now? Living "with many creatures, little and large," in central Mexico.

ACADEMIC LANGUAGE HANDBOOK

Use the academic language frames in this handbook as a reference during academic discussions.

The **heading** states the overall type of discussion or interaction.

Look for the **"If" statement** that most closely describes the specific type of interaction.

Look for examples of completed frames in **speech bubbles**.

Facilitating Discussion
Collaborate to have a discussion in a small group.

If you want to ask a group member to add an idea . . .
- So, _____, what do you think?
- So, _____, what's your (experience/suggestion)?
- So, _____, what is your perspective?
- _____, what idea did you (come up with/generate)?
- _____, what idea can you add?

If you want to ask a group member about a word . . .
- So _____, are you familiar with the word _____?

If you want to share word knowledge with the group . . .
- I've never seen or heard the word _____.
- I recognize the word _____ but need to learn how to use it.
- I can use _____ in a sentence. For example, _____.
- I know that the word _____ means _____.

If you want to share word knowledge with the class . . .
- We are unfamiliar with the word _____.
- We recognize the word _____, but we would benefit from a review of what it means and how to use it.
- We think _____ means _____.

> *I've never seen or heard the word "nutrition."*

Language Tip
Follow "For example, . . ." with a sentence that shows you are familiar with the word. You could say, "I can use *nutrition* in a sentence. For example, *fruits and vegetables are important for nutrition.*"

Stating Perspectives
Give your opinion about an issue or a topic.

If you want to share your opinion . . .
- Based on my experience, _____.
- In my (opinion/experience), _____.
- From my (perspective/point of view) _____.
- I (would argue/maintain) that _____.
- I have observed that _____.

> *Based on my experience, students sometimes throw away cafeteria food.*

Introducing Evidence
Provide supporting evidence for your claim.

If you want to give text evidence . . .
- For (example/instance), _____.
- To illustrate, _____.
- As an illustration, _____.
- In the text, _____.
- The (text/author) _____.
- In addition, the text _____.
- The data (show/prove) _____.
- (Studies/Recent findings) (show/prove) _____.

Language Tip
Complete the frame "The (text/author) . . ." with a citation verb, such as "reports" or "states." Then add text evidence to support your claim. For example, "The author reports that junk food bans would encourage healthy eating habits."

Responding to Evidence
Share your response to data or statistics.

If evidence gets your attention . . .
- One finding that caught my attention is _____ because _____.
- One surprising statistic is that _____.
- One statistic that didn't surprise me at all is _____ because _____.
- A piece of data that caught my attention is that _____.

Read the **Language Tips** to help you understand challenging language and how to complete frames with correct grammar.

Choose a **frame** to structure what you say. A **blank line** means that you need to complete the sentence. **Words in parentheses** mean you have a choice of using one of the words or phrases listed.

Requesting Assistance

Ask the teacher or a classmate for help.

If you don't understand what the speaker said . . .

- I couldn't hear you. Could you repeat that?
- I didn't hear you. Please repeat your (idea/response).

If you don't understand what the speaker meant . . .

- I don't quite understand. Could you give me an example?
- I am somewhat confused. Could you explain that again?
- I am not sure I get your point. Could you explain what you mean by _____?

> ### Language Tip
> In formal settings, avoid saying "huh?" or "I don't get it" when you don't understand. Instead, politely say, "I am somewhat confused. Could you explain that again?"

Asking for Clarification

Ask for more information.

If you have a question . . .

- I have a question about _____.
- One question I have is _____?

If you need information repeated . . .

- Will you explain _____ again?

> Will you explain the directions for this assignment again?

If you need more explanation . . .

- What do you mean by _____?
- I don't quite understand your (question/suggestion).
- What exactly do you mean by _____?
- Could you explain what you mean by _____?

> What exactly do you mean by "the topic sentence"?

Facilitating Discussion

Collaborate to have a discussion in a small group.

If you want to ask a group member to add an idea . . .

- So, _____, what do you think?
- So, _____, what's your (experience/suggestion)?
- So, _____, what is your perspective?
- _____, what idea did you (come up with/ generate)?
- _____, what idea can you add?

If you want to ask a group member about a word . . .

- So _____, are you familiar with the word _____?

I've never seen or heard the word "obesity."

If you want to share word knowledge with the group . . .

- I've never seen or heard the word _____.
- I recognize the word _____ but need to learn how to use it.
- I can use _____ in a sentence. For example, _____.
- I know that the word _____ means _____.

If you want to share word knowledge with the class . . .

- We are unfamiliar with the word _____.
- We recognize the word _____, but we would benefit from a review of what it means and how to use it.
- We think _____ means _____.

Language Tip

Follow "For example, . . ." with a sentence that shows you are familiar with the word.

You could say, "I can use nutrition in a sentence. For example, fruits and vegetables are important for nutrition."

Stating Perspectives

Give your opinion about an issue or a topic.

If you want to share your opinion . . .

- Based on my experience, _____.
- In my (opinion/experience), _____.
- From my (perspective/point of view) _____.
- I (would argue/maintain) that _____.
- I have observed that _____.

> Based on my experience, students sometimes throw away cafeteria food.

Introducing Evidence

Provide supporting evidence for your claim.

If you want to give text evidence . . .

- For (example/instance), _____.
- To illustrate, _____.
- As an illustration, _____.
- In the text, _____.
- The (text/author) _____.
- In addition, the text _____.
- The data (show/prove) _____.
- (Studies/Recent findings) (show/prove) _____.

> **Language Tip**
>
> Complete the frame "The (text/author) . . ." with a citation verb, such as "reports" or "states." Then add text evidence to support your claim.
>
> For example, "The author reports that junk food bans would encourage healthy eating habits."

Responding to Evidence

Share your response to data or statistics.

If evidence gets your attention . . .

- One finding that caught my attention is _____ because _____.
- One surprising statistic is that _____.
- One statistic that didn't surprise me at all is _____ because _____.
- A piece of data that caught my attention is that _____.

Elaborating

Provide more information and details to support a claim.

> **Language Tip**
>
> "Instance" is a noun that is another way of saying "example." "Illustrate" is a verb that means to show or give an example.

If you want to give an example . . .

- For example, _____.
- For instance, _____.
- As an example, _____.
- Specifically, _____.
- In particular, _____.
- As an illustration, _____.
- To illustrate, _____.
- To demonstrate, _____.
- In my experience, _____.

> I know this because my friend who plays basketball has to eat before practice.

If you want to share a personal experience . . .

- I know this because _____.
- It has been my experience that _____.
- I have found that _____.
- I have noticed that _____.
- I have discovered that _____.
- I have observed that _____.
- Based on my experience, _____.
- Personally, _____.

If you want to provide a reason . . .

- The reason I know this is _____.
- This is the case because _____.
- The main cause of this is _____.

Restating Ideas

Listen carefully and repeat classmates' ideas in your own words.

If you want to restate someone else's idea . . .

* So you think that _____.
* So what you're saying is that _____.
* So what you're suggesting is that _____.
* So your (opinion/perspective) is that _____.
* If I understand you correctly, your opinion is that _____.
* So if I understand you correctly, your point of view is that _____.
* In other words, you have observed that _____.
* In other words, your point of view is that _____.
* In other words, your stance is that _____.

> ### Language Tip
>
> Complete each frame with an independent clause that restates your classmate's idea in your own words.
>
> For example, "So your perspective is that our school should start an after-school running club."

If someone restates your idea correctly . . .

* Yes, that's (right/correct).
* Yes, that's accurate.

If someone restates your idea incorrectly . . .

* No, not (really/exactly). What I meant was _____.
* Actually, what I meant was _____.
* No, not quite. What I meant was _____.
* No. What I intended to say was _____.

> Actually, what I meant was a salad bar could encourage students to eat more vegetables.

Agreeing & Disagreeing

Politely tell others if you agree or disagree with their ideas.

I agree with Erik's point of view about vending machines in schools.

If you agree with an idea . . .

- I agree with _____'s idea.
- I agree with _____'s opinion.
- I completely agree with _____'s perspective.
- I agree with _____'s point of view about _____.

If you disagree with an idea . . .

- I don't agree with _____'s idea.
- I disagree with _____'s opinion.
- I completely disagree with _____'s perspective.
- I disagree with _____'s point of view about _____.

If you are undecided about an idea . . .

- I'm undecided about _____'s idea.
- I'm uncertain about _____'s idea.
- I'm unconvinced about _____'s idea.
- I'm unsure about _____'s idea.
- I see both sides of the issue.
- I can't definitively agree or disagree with _____'s idea.
- I am undecided whether _____.
- I am more inclined to believe that _____.
- I remain unconvinced that _____.
- I need to consider the idea of _____ further.

Language Tip

When you "definitively" agree or disagree with something, your opinion cannot be changed.

Comparing Ideas

Discuss how your ideas are similar to or different from others' ideas.

If your idea is similar . . .

- My (experience/belief) is similar to _____'s.
- My observation is similar to _____'s.
- My point of view is related to _____'s.
- My stance is similar to _____'s.
- I see it the same way as _____.
- My reaction was similar to _____'s. I was also (impressed/surprised) by _____.
- Like _____, I appreciated the way the (speaker/writer) _____.
- _____ and I had similar (experiences/initial reactions).

Language Tip

An "observation" is something you have seen or noticed.

Your "stance" on an issue is your position.

If your idea is different . . .

- My (experience/belief) is different from _____'s.
- My observation is different from _____'s.
- My stance is different from _____'s.
- I see it differently from _____.
- _____ and I had somewhat different (experiences/initial reactions).

My observation is different from Jess's.

Collaborating With Others

Discuss responses with a partner or group members.

Language Tip

When you are working with a partner or in a small group, ask others to share ideas by saying, "What are your thoughts?"

We could also write the example "fresh produce."

If you want to ask a partner or group member to respond . . .

- What should we write?
- What do you think?
- Let's think about what to write.
- What are your thoughts?
- Do you agree?
- Do you have any ideas?
- What's your opinion?
- Let's focus on what to write.
- Do you have a different opinion?

If you want to share your response with a partner or group member . . .

- We could put _____.
- We could also write _____.
- A good option might be _____.
- We could also try _____.
- (One/Another) option is _____.
- (One/Another) idea I have is _____.

If you want to agree on an idea . . .

- Okay. Let's write _____.

Reporting Ideas

Share ideas during a class discussion.

If you are reporting responses . . .

- We thought of _____.
- We selected _____.
- We agreed upon _____.
- We came up with _____.
- We chose _____.
- We decided upon _____
- We came to a consensus on _____.

If you are choosing precise words . . .

- We would like to (suggest/recommend/propose) the precise word _____.
- We (decided/agreed) upon the precise word

    _____.
- We selected the precise word _____.
- We came to a consensus on the precise word _____.
- One precise word we (identified/considered/proposed) is _____.
- One precise word we selected is _____.

> We would like to propose the precise word "obesity."

If you are selecting someone else to report . . .

- I choose _____.
- I select _____.
- I'd like to hear from _____.
- I nominate _____.
- I'd appreciate a response from _____.
- I'd welcome a contribution from _____.

Language Tip

When you "come to a consensus" with your group members, it means that you all agree on the response.

Summarizing

State the key ideas and details of a text.

A central idea in this text is that some people support allowing students to make their own food choices.

If you want to state the key idea . . .

- The key idea of this text is _____.
- The author's main idea is _____.
- The text is primarily about _____.
- This text focuses on _____.
- The author's main point is _____.
- A central idea in this text is _____.

If you want to describe key details . . .

- (One/Another) important detail is _____.
- (One/Another) key detail in this text is _____.
- (One/An additional) essential detail is _____.
- (One/Another) significant detail is _____.
- (One/Another) relevant supporting detail is _____.
- (One/Another) vital detail is _____.
- Perhaps the most (important/significant/relevant) detail in this text is _____.

Language Tip

Choose a precise adjective that fits the detail you describe:

- An "essential" detail proves a point or supports a topic.
- A "significant" detail has an important influence or effect on the topic or issue.
- A "relevant" detail is related to your position.

Paraphrasing

Restate and explain an author's ideas in your own words.

If you want to restate an author's idea . . .

- To put it another way, _____.
- To paraphrase, _____.
- In other words, _____.
- In this quote, the author states _____.
- In this quote, the author makes a case for _____.

If you want to explain what an author means . . .

- This quote reinforces the idea that _____.
- This quote clarifies that _____.
- The author seems to be saying that _____.
- This quote makes it evident that _____.

> **Language Tip**
>
> Paraphrase ideas when you summarize texts. Also, paraphrase evidence that supports your claim when you write a justification or argument.
>
> For example, "In other words, selling snacks can have a significant financial impact."

This quote reinforces the idea that eating junk food can have serious consequences.

Affirming Ideas

Acknowledge a classmate's idea before stating your own idea.

Language Tip

Acknowledge that a classmate had something valuable to say. Then use a transition such as "however" or "I also think" to state your own perspective.

If you want to acknowledge others' ideas . . .

- That's an interesting claim.
- I hadn't thought of that.
- That's an interesting opinion.
- I can understand why you see it this way.
- That's an intriguing perspective.
- That's a compelling point of view.

Negotiating

Persuade others and support your opinions.

I heard you say that our school should start a running club, and I haven't thought about that before.

If you want to provide a counterargument . . .

- I agree with _____, but I wonder _____.
- I heard you say _____. However, _____.

If you want to acknowledge perspectives . . .

- I heard you say _____, and (Name) just pointed out _____.
- I heard you say _____, and I haven't thought about that before.
- I heard you say _____, and that's a good point. I still think _____, though, because _____.

Offering Feedback

Share your feedback and suggestions about a classmate's writing or speech.

If you want to give positive feedback . . .

* I appreciate how you used _____.
* I appreciate how you included _____.
* I appreciate how you explained _____.
* You did an effective job of using _____.
* You did an effective job of including _____.
* You did an effective job of explaining _____.
* I appreciated the specific example of _____ that you included.
* Your concrete detail(s) about _____ strengthened your response.
* Your use of _____ was skillful.

Language Tip

Complete the frames with a noun phrase to give positive feedback.

For example, "You did an effective job of including transitions to connect your ideas."

If you want to offer a suggestion . . .

* As you revise your (writing/speech), focus on including _____.
* As you revise your (writing/speech), focus on improving _____.
* As you revise your (writing/speech), focus on explaining _____.
* Your (writing/speech) will be stronger if you include _____.
* Your (writing/speech) will be stronger if you improve _____.
* Your (writing/speech) will be stronger if you explain _____.
* I think you misspelled the word _____.
* Adding _____ would make your response (clearer/stronger).

As you revise your argument, focus on including relevant text evidence to support your claim.

Vocabulary to Analyze Context

Use these terms to analyze context and word parts as clues to word meaning.

analyze

verb to carefully examine something to understand it

analysis

noun a careful examination of something to understand it

context

noun the language surrounding a word or phrase that helps you understand it

prefix

noun a group of letters added to the beginning of a word to change its meaning

mis + *understand* = *misunderstand*

suffix

noun a letter or group of letters added to the end of a word that changes the part of speech

polite (adjective) + *ness* = *politeness (noun)*

base word

noun a word that is used as a base to create other words by adding a prefix or suffix

un + *think* + *able* = *unthinkable*

root word

noun a word or word part that comes from another language, such as Greek or Latin

auto + *mobile* = *automobile*

Common Prefixes & Suffixes

Learn these affixes to use as clues to the meanings of unfamiliar words.

Prefix	Meaning	Example Words
anti–	against	antiperspirant, antisocial
dis–	not, opposite of	disagree, disapprove
im–, in–	not	immature, incorrect
inter–	between	international, interactive
mis–	bad, wrong	miscalculate, misunderstand
non–, un–	not	nonviolence, unable, unbroken
pre–	before	prepay, precede
re–	again	reread, reconsider
sub–	below, under	submarine, subtitle
trans–	across	transaction, transport

Suffix	Meaning	Example Words
–able, –ible *(adj)*	having a particular quality; something that is possible	comparable, valuable, accessible
–ate *(verb)*	to make, cause, or act	communicate, regulate
–ation, –ion *(noun)*	the act or result of doing something	preparation, multiplication, contribution, determination
–er, –or *(noun)*	someone who does	manager, organizer, investigator, mentor
–ful *(adj)*	full of	doubtful, harmful
–ity *(noun)*	having a particular quality	capacity, identity, productivity
–ive *(adj)*	having a particular quality	collaborative, productive, talkative
–less *(adj)*	without	careless, powerless
–ly *(adv)*	to happen in a particular way	accurately, certainly, lastly
–ment *(noun)*	the result	achievement, investment, requirement

Use the descriptions and transitions in this handbook as a reference for your academic writing assignments.

Justification

*A **justification** states a claim and supports it with logical reasons and relevant evidence.*

A. The **topic sentence** clearly states the writer's claim about the issue.

B. **Detail sentences** support the claim with reasons and evidence from texts and the writer's experiences.

C. The **concluding sentence** restates the writer's claim about the issue.

D. **Transition words or phrases** introduce evidence and connect ideas.

Topic Sentence
Reason 1
Evidence
Reason 2
Evidence
Concluding Sentence

Transitions

Use these transitions to introduce evidence when you write a justification.

- Evidence shows _____.
- For example, _____.
- In fact, _____.
- _____ also _____.
- Additionally, _____.

Formal Summary

*A **formal written summary** is a type of informative writing. It provides an objective overview of the topic and important details from an informational text. The writer credits the author, but writes mostly in his or her own words, without including personal opinions.*

A. The **topic sentence** includes the text type, title, author, and topic.

B. **Detail sentences** include the important details from the summarized text.

C. The **concluding sentence** restates the author's conclusion in the writer's own words.

D. **Transition words or phrases** help the reader identify the most important details.

Topic Sentence
Important Detail 1
Important Detail 2
Important Detail 3
Concluding Sentence

Transitions

Use these transitions to help the reader identify the most important details of your formal written summary.

- First, _____.
- In addition, _____.
- Furthermore, _____.

- _____ also _____.
- Finally, _____.

Summary & Response

A **summary and response** *provides an objective overview of the topic and important details from a text, then presents the writer's position.*

A. The **summary** includes a topic sentence, detail sentences, and a concluding sentence.

B. The **response** includes a transitional sentence, a topic sentence that presents the writer's position, supporting details, and a final statement.

Summary

Topic Sentence
Important Details
Concluding Sentence

Response

Transitional Sentence
Topic Sentence
Reasons and Evidence
Final Statement

Transitions

Use these transitions to organize the details of your summary and response.

- Initially, _____.
- To begin with, _____.
- The writer continues to _____.

- Additionally, _____.
- Finally, _____.

Argument

*An **argument** states a claim, then supports it with logical reasons and relevant evidence from sources.*

A. The **introduction** clearly states the writer's claim about the issue.

B. **Detail paragraphs** support the claim with reasons and evidence. The writer may also present counterclaims and respond with strong evidence.

C. The **conclusion** strongly restates the writer's claim about the issue.

D. **Transition words or phrases** connect ideas.

Introduction	
Reason 1	
Evidence	
Reason 2	
Evidence	
Conclusion	

Transitions

Use these transitions to connect ideas in your argument.

- A key reason _____.
- For example, _____.
- Another major reason _____.

- One interesting point is _____.
- However, _____.

Informative Text

*An **informative text** examines a topic and conveys ideas and information.*

A. The **introduction** contains a thesis statement that tells what the writer will explain about the topic.

B. **Important details** develop the topic with text evidence. Evidence can include facts, statistics, examples, or quotations.

C. The **conclusion** sums up and restates the thesis about the topic.

D. **Transition words or phrases** help the reader identify the most important details.

Introduction
Important Detail 1
Important Detail 2
Important Detail 3
Conclusion

Transitions

Use transitions to help the reader identify the most important details in your informative text.

- Because _____.
- Another (effect/impact/ consequence) of _____ is _____.
- Due to _____.

- As a result of _____.
- However, _____.
- In contrast to _____.

Narrative

*A **narrative** tells a story from a clear point of view. Narratives can be experiences written from someone's own life.*

A. The **topic sentence** clearly identifies the purpose of the narrative.

B. **Detail sentences** show the order of events using action verbs and sensory details, such as precise adjectives and adverbs.

C. The **conclusion** explains the importance of the story.

D. **Transition words or phrases** help move the reader through the events of the story.

Topic Sentence	
Sensory Detail 1	
Sensory Detail 2	
Sensory Detail 3	
Conclusion	

Transitions

Use these transitions to help move the reader through the events of your narrative.

- First, _____.
- At that time _____.
- Suddenly, _____.

- (Since then/later) _____.

ACADEMIC GLOSSARY

A glossary is a useful tool found at the back of many books. It contains information about key words in the text. Review the sample glossary entry below.

This is an **entry word**—the word you look up. It is divided into syllables. Words in bold are Words to Know and words highlighted in yellow are Words to Go or Concept Words.

The **pronunciation** comes after the entry word. Letters and letter combinations stand for different sounds. The stressed syllable is marked in bold letters.

The **meaning** of the word follows the part of speech.

The **part of speech** follows the pronunciation.

A **number** appears at the beginning of each meaning if more than one meaning is given for the entry word.

The **Spanish cognate** is a word that looks or sounds the same in Spanish and has a similar meaning.

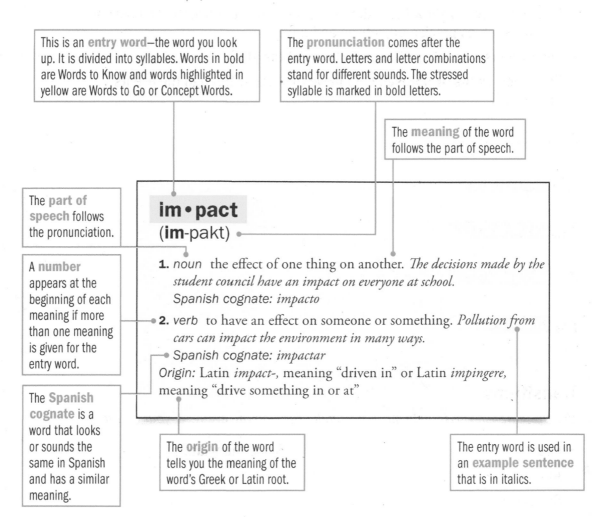

im•pact
(**im**-pakt)

1. *noun* the effect of one thing on another. *The decisions made by the student council have an impact on everyone at school.*
   Spanish cognate: *impacto*

2. *verb* to have an effect on someone or something. *Pollution from cars can impact the environment in many ways.*
   Spanish cognate: *impactar*
   Origin: Latin *impact-*, meaning "driven in" or Latin *impingere*, meaning "drive something in or at"

The **origin** of the word tells you the meaning of the word's Greek or Latin root.

The entry word is used in an **example sentence** that is in italics.

ad•dic•ted
(uh-**dik**-tid)

adjective unable to give something up. *My brother is totally addicted to science-fiction movies.*
Spanish cognate: *adicto(a)*

ad•dic•tion
(uh-**dik**-shuhn)

noun the physical or emotional need to do something that is harmful on a regular basis. *My dad is trying to quit smoking and break his addiction to cigarettes.*
Origin: Latin *addicere,* meaning "assign"
Spanish cognate: *adicción*

ad•dic•tive
(uh-**dik**-tiv)

adjective hard to give up. *Surprisingly, many prescription drugs are highly addictive.*
Spanish cognate: *adictivo(a)*

ad•mire
(ad-**mire**)

verb to like someone or something's qualities. *Many people admire the skills of Olympic athletes.*
Origin: Latin *ad-,* meaning "at" + *mirari,* meaning "wonder"
Spanish cognate: *admirar*

ad•mit
(ad-**mit**)

verb to accept or announce information as true. *I have to admit that you did an amazing job putting together and painting this model car.*
Origin: Latin *ad-,* meaning "to" + *mittere,* meaning "send"
Spanish cognate: *admitir*

a•dore
(uh-**dor**)

verb to show great fondness or devotion. *Scamp and Rusty, our two dogs, adore us and would do anything for us.*
Origin: Latin *adorare,* meaning "to worship"
Spanish cognate: *adorar*

a•dor•ing•ly
(uh-**dor**-ing-lee)

adverb in a way that shows great fondness or devotion. *As they said their wedding vows, the bride and groom looked adoringly at each other.*
Origin: Latin *adorare,* meaning "to worship"
Spanish cognate: *con adoración*

af•fect
(uh-**fekt**)

verb to change someone or something. *A well-written song is likely to affect many people.*
Origin: Latin *afficere,* meaning "to influence"
Spanish cognate: *afectar*

af•fil•i•a•tion
(uh-fil-ee-**ay**-shuhn)

noun membership in or close connection with something. *Some people have an affiliation with a church, synagogue, or other religious body.*
Origin: Latin *ad-,* meaning "toward" + *filius,* meaning "son"
Spanish cognate: *afiliación, filiación*

al•ba•tross
(**al**-buh-tross)

noun a large seabird that is able to fly for a long time and has webbed feet and long wings. *Out at sea, sailors watched an albatross as it flew by their ship.*
Spanish cognate: *albatros*

ACADEMIC GLOSSARY

al•ter•na•tive
(awl-**tur**-nuh-tiv)

noun something you can choose instead of something else. *It is important to consider every possible alternative before making a big decision like changing schools.*
Origin: Latin *alter*, meaning "other"
Spanish cognate: *alternativa*

ap•peal
(uh-**peel**)

verb to be likeable or interesting. *Action movies are popular because they appeal to many people.*
Origin: Latin *ad-*, meaning "to" + *pellere*, meaning "to drive"

ap•peal•ing
(uh-**peel**-ing)

adjective likeable or interesting. *Cookies smell very appealing when they come right out of the oven.*

ar•tis•tic
(ar-**tiss**-tik)

adjective good at drawing or painting; done with skill or imagination. *My teacher liked my abstract drawing and told me I was very artistic.*
Origin: Latin *ars*, *art-*, meaning "art"
Spanish cognate: *artístico(a)*

as•sess
(uh-**sess**)

verb to look at an event in order to learn from it. *After the last performance of the school play, we will all get together to assess how well we did.*
Origin: Latin *ad-*, meaning "to, at" + *sedere*, meaning "sit"

a•vail•a•ble
(uh-**vayl**-luh-buhl)

adjective possible to get or be used; unoccupied or not busy. *Our teacher is always available after school to give students extra help.*

ban
(**ban**)

noun an order that says something is not allowed. *The principal announced a ban on junk food in school vending machines.*

ben•e•fi•cial
(ben-uh-**fish**-uhl)

adjective having a good or helpful effect on something. *Recycling is very beneficial to the environment.*
Spanish cognate: *beneficioso(a)*

ben•e•fit
(**ben**-uh-fit)

verb to help or be helped by something or someone. *Everyone could benefit from getting a good night's sleep and eating plenty of vegetables.*
Origin: Latin *bene*, meaning "well" + *facere*, meaning "do"
Spanish cognate: *beneficiar*

bond
(**bond**)

noun a close connection with or strong feeling for someone. *I always will have a close bond with Dana, my first really good friend.*

bor•der
(**bor**-dur)

noun the dividing line between two countries or regions. *Montana, Minnesota, and Maine are three states that are on the border of Canada.*

cal•o•rie

(**kal**-uh-ree)

noun a unit of energy produced by food. *If you're trying to lose weight, every calorie counts toward achieving your goal.*
Origin: Latin *calor*, meaning "heat"
Spanish cognate: *caloría*

chip in

(chip **in**)

verb phrase to contribute money toward a shared goal. *Sanjay was eager to chip in so that we could buy Susanna a really nice birthday present.*

cho•rus

(**kor**-uhss)

noun the part of a song a singer repeats after each verse. *Do you know the chorus of the song "Waltzing Matilda"?*
Origin: Greek *khoros*, meaning "band of singers or dancers"

chron•i•cle

(**kron**-uh-kuhl)

verb to describe events the way they really happened. *These books chronicle the early history of Great Britain.*
Origin: Greek *khronikos*, meaning "of time"

code

(**kode**)

noun a set of rules that tell people how to behave. *People in the military live by a strict code of honor.*
Origin: Latin *codex, codic-*, meaning "book"
Spanish cognate: *código*

col•lab•o•rate

(kuh-**lab**-uh-rate)

verb to work together to do something. *Kenton, Alejandro, and Amy will collaborate to create an act for the school's talent show.*
Origin: Latin *col-*, meaning "together" + *laborare*, meaning "to work"
Spanish cognate: *colaborar*

com•mu•ni•cate

(kuh-**myoo**-nuh-kate)

verb to share information or ideas with others. *Most of my friends use texting to communicate quickly and effectively.*
Origin: Latin *communis*, meaning "shared"
Spanish cognate: *comunicar, comunicarse*

com•mu•ni•ca•tion

(kuh-myoo-nuh-**kay**-shuhn)

noun the act of sharing information or expressing thoughts and feelings with someone. *My cell phone helps me stay in communication with my friends and my parents.*
Spanish cognate: *comunicación*

com•mu•ni•ca•tive

(kuh-**myoo**-nuh-kuh-tiv)

adjective able and even eager to share information, thoughts, and feelings. *I am more communicative with my parents now that I am older.*
Spanish cognate: *comunicativo(a)*

com•mu•ni•ty

(kuh-**myoo**-nuh-tee)

noun a group of people who live in an area; the area where a group of people live. *I look forward to the festival our thriving community sponsors every summer.*
Origin: Latin *communis*, meaning "shared"
Spanish cognate: *comunidad*

ACADEMIC GLOSSARY

com•pli•cat•ed
(**kom**-pli-kay-tid)
adjective difficult to understand; having many different parts or ideas. *The math problems were very complicated, but Eric solved them all.*
Origin: Latin *com-*, meaning "together" + *plicare*, meaning "to fold"
Spanish cognate: *complicado(a)*

con•cise
(kuh-**sisse**)
adjective saying a lot in a few words. *Each student gave a concise report about the novel that he or she had read.*
Origin: Latin *concidere*, meaning "cut up, cut down"
Spanish cognate: *conciso(a)*

con•nect
(kuh-**nekt**)
verb to join one thing with another. *You must connect this cord to a power source if you want the device to work.*
Origin: Latin *con-*, meaning "together" + *nectere*, meaning "bind"
Spanish cognate: *conectar*

con•nec•tion
(kuh-**nek**-shuhn)
noun a link between things, such as objects, people, or ideas. *Brad made a strong connection with Jamal when he found out that they liked the same comic books.*
Spanish cognate: *conexión*

con•stant
(**kon**-stuhnt)
adjective happening all the time. *Aunt Jennifer seems to have a constant smile on her face.*
Origin: Latin *con-*, meaning "with" + *stare*, meaning "stand"
Spanish cognate: *constante*

con•struc•tive
(kuh-**struhk**-tiv)
adjective useful for improvement on a project or an issue. *With constructive advice from Mr. Kowalski, our group put together a great multimedia presentation.*
Origin: Latin *con-*, meaning "together" + *struere*, meaning "pile, build"
Spanish cognate: *constructivo(a)*

con•struc•tive•ly
(kuh-**struhk**-tiv-lee)
adverb in a way that is helpful and useful. *After playing a video game for almost an hour, Allie decided to use her time more constructively.*
Spanish cognate: *constructivamente*

con•sum•er
(kuh-**soo**-mur)
noun someone who buys or uses products and services. *This supermarket offers consumers a discount if they bring their own reusable bags.*
Spanish cognate: *consumidor*

con•ven•ience
(kuh-**vee**-nyuhnss)
noun something that makes a person's life easier. *Everyone in the family loves the convenience of a microwave oven.*
Origin: Latin *convenient-*, meaning "assembling, agreeing"
Spanish cognate: *conveniencia*

con•ven•ient
(kuhn-**vee**-nyuhnt)

adjective easy to have or access. *What would be a convenient time for us to get together to plan our history project?*
Spanish cognate: *conveniente*

co•or•di•na•tion
(ko-or-dih-**nay**-shuhn)

noun the ability to use parts of the body or other items so that they work together. *Circus performers need a lot of coordination to juggle or swing on a trapeze.*
Origin: Latin *co-*, meaning "with, together" + *ordo, ordin-*, meaning "order"

coun•sel•ing
(**koun**-suh-ling)

noun advice given to people about their problems. *My older sister will seek some counseling about choosing a college.*
Origin: Latin *consilium*, meaning "consultation, advice"

coun•sel•or
(**koun**-suh-lur)

noun someone who offers help with problems. *After Yoni talked to the school counselor, he felt better.*
Spanish cognate: *consejero*

cre•a•tive
(kree-**ay**-tiv)

adjective involving the use of imagination to create something new. *Maria made some very creative choices when she designed this poster.*
Origin: Latin *creat-*, meaning "produced"
Spanish cognate: *creativo(a)*

cre•a•tiv•i•ty
(kree-ay-**tiv**-uh-tee)

noun the ability to use imagination to think of new ideas. *I feel that Sean, with his great creativity, will be a famous artist one day.*
Spanish cognate: *creatividad*

cri•sis
(**krye**-siss)

noun a time of severe emotional difficulty or danger. *Our class was faced with a crisis when our teacher became seriously ill.*
Origin: Greek *krisis*, meaning "decision"
Spanish cognate: *crisis*

crit•ic
(**krit**-ik)

noun someone who judges something. *The movie critic gave a bitterly negative review of the new film.*
Origin: Greek *kritēs*, meaning "a judge"
Spanish cognate: *crítico(a)*

crit•i•cism
(**krit**-uh-siz-uhm)

noun remarks that say what you think is bad or incorrect about something. *After we gave our presentation, the teacher offered some fair and helpful criticism.*
Origin: Latin *criticus*, meaning "judge, decide" + *-ism*
Spanish cognate: *crítica*

crum•bly
(**kruhm**-blee)

adjective easily broken into small pieces. *This slice of bread has dried out and now is very crumbly.*

ACADEMIC GLOSSARY

cul•tur•al
(**kuhl**-chur-uhl)
adjective having to do with the art, ideas, and beliefs of a group of people. *Many families in my neighborhood have strong cultural traditions.*
Spanish cognate: *cultural*

cul•ture
(**kuhl**-chur)
noun the way of life shared by people in a particular place or society. *Mrs. Hayes taught us about the culture of the ancient Aztecs.*
Origin: Latin *colere*, meaning "tend, cultivate" + *-al*
Spanish cognate: *cultura*

dam•age
(**dam**-ij)
1. *verb* to harm or spoil something or someone. *Shipping those dishes without proper padding could badly damage them.*
2. *noun* the harm caused by something. *Towns along the seacoast suffered severe damage from the hurricane.*
Origin: Latin *damnum*, meaning "loss or hurt"

de•bris
(duh-**bree**)
noun scattered pieces of something that has been broken or destroyed. *After the flood, it took weeks to get rid of all the debris.*

de•cline
(dee-**kline**)
noun a decrease in the quality, quantity, or importance of something. *During flu season, our school usually sees a decline in attendance.*
Origin: Latin *de-*, meaning "down" + *clinare*, meaning "to bend"

de•com•pose
(dee-kuhm-**poze**)
verb to rot or decay. *The leaves that fall onto the forest floor will decompose and enrich the soil.*
Origin: Latin *de-*, meaning "the opposite of" + *com-*, meaning "together" + *ponere*, meaning "to put or place"
Spanish cognate: *descomponerse*

de•face
(di-**fayss**)
verb to destroy or damage the way something looks. *It is a crime to deface other people's property.*

dem•on•strate
(**dem**-uhn-strate)
verb to show a particular ability, quality, or feeling. *Some sports fans demonstrate their loyalty to the home team by wearing the team's colors.*
Origin: Latin *demonstrat-*, meaning "pointed out"
Spanish cognate: *demostrar*

de•te•ri•o•rate
(di-**tihr**-ee-uh-rate)
verb to get worse. *If you don't follow the doctor's advice, your health will begin to deteriorate.*
Origin: Latin *deterior*, meaning "worse"
Spanish cognate: *deteriorarse*

di•lem•ma
(duh-**lem**-uh)
noun a problem, often involving a difficult choice. *I have a dilemma: Should I miss the game to work on my report or go to the game and stay up late to work on my report?*
Origin: Greek *di-*, meaning "two" + *lēmma*, meaning "premise"
Spanish cognate: *dilema*

dis•pose
(dis-**pohz**)
verb to use something briefly and throw it away. *Let's use these bags to dispose of the rubbish from our picnic.*
Origin: Latin *disponere,* meaning "arrange"
Spanish cognate: *disponer*

dis•tract
(diss-**trakt**)
verb to take someone's attention away from what he or she is doing. *We tried not to let the barking dog distract us from our homework.*
Origin: Latin *dis-,* meaning "apart" + *trahere,* meaning "to draw, drag"
Spanish cognate: *distraer*

du•ra•ble
(**dur**-uh-buhl)
adjective tough and able to last for a long time. *These blue jeans are so durable that they never seem to wear out.*
Origin: Latin *durare,* meaning "to last"
Spanish cognate: *duradero(a)*

e•lab•o•rate•ly
(i-**lab**-ur-it-lee)
adverb in a complicated, detailed, often showy way. *No one at the party could stop looking at Juliana's elaborately decorated costume.*
Origin: Latin *elaborat-,* meaning "worked out"
Spanish cognate: *elaboradamente*

e•lim•i•nate
(i-**lim**-uh-nate)
verb to completely get rid of something. *Because of her allergies, MaKayla must eliminate peanuts from her diet.*
Origin: Latin *e-,* meaning "out" + *limen, limin,* meaning "threshold"
Spanish cognate: *eliminar*

em•phat•ic
(em-**fat**-ik)
adjective forceful and strong, in order to show the importance of an idea. *Jake's piano teacher is emphatic about having him practice his lesson every day.*
Origin: Greek *em-,* meaning "in" + *phainein,* meaning "to show"
Spanish cognate: *enfático(a)*

em•phat•i•cal•ly
(em-**fat**-ik-lee)
adverb doing or saying something with great energy or excitement. *When her favorite songs come on the radio, Mom emphatically sings along.*
Spanish cognate: *enfáticamente*

en•chant•ed
(en-**chan**-tid)
adjective changed by magic or something beautiful. *The audience was enchanted by the singer's amazing voice and moving songs.*
Origin: Latin *in-,* meaning "in" + *cantare,* meaning "sing"
Spanish cognate: *encantado(a)*

en•vi•ron•ment
(en-**vye**-ruhn-muhnt)
noun natural surroundings such as the air, land, or sea. *In order to help keep the environment clean, I always try to pick up garbage I see on the ground.*

en•vi•ron•ment•al
(en-vye-ruhn-**mehn**-tuhl)
adjective concerning the conditions of the place where you are. *Which kind of pollution do you think creates the greatest environmental damage in our community?*

ACADEMIC GLOSSARY

en•vi•ron•ment•al•ist
(en-vye-ruhn-**mehn**-tuhl-ist)
noun a person who studies the conditions in which things live and who tries to keep those conditions as natural as possible. *At the assembly, the environmentalist told us how the choices we make have an impact on other living things.*

ep•i•dem•ic
(ep-uh-**dem**-ik)
noun a sudden outbreak of a disease or other condition that spreads quickly. *Every winter the flu epidemic hits our school and forces many students to stay home.*
Origin: Greek *epi,* meaning "upon" + *dēmos,* meaning "the people"
Spanish cognate: *epidemia*

ex•pen•sive
(ek-**spen**-siv)
adjective costing a lot of money. *Leah had to mow two dozen lawns to earn enough money to pay for her expensive new jacket.*
Origin: Latin *ex-,* meaning "out" + *pendere,* meaning "weigh, pay" + *-ive*

ex•press
(ek-**spress**)
verb to tell or show what you are thinking or feeling by using words or actions. *I like to express my feelings by drawing pictures.*
Origin: Latin *ex-,* meaning "out" + *pressare,* meaning "to press"
Spanish cognate: *expresar*

ex•pres•sion
(ek-**spresh**-uhn)
noun the look on someone's face that shows what he or she is feeling or thinking. *The expression on David's face clearly showed that he was surprised by the party.*
Spanish cognate: *expresión*

ex•tinct
(ek-**stingkt**)
adjective died out; no longer having any living members. *Jon would love to see living dinosaurs; unfortunately, dinosaurs are extinct.*
Origin: Latin *exstinct-,* meaning "extinguished"
Spanish cognate: *extinto(a)*

fauns
(**fawnz**)
noun mythological characters who were said to be part human and part goat. *Mr. Tumnus is the most famous of the fauns in* The Chronicles of Narnia.
Spanish cognate: *faunos*

fi•nan•cial
(fye-**nan**-shuhl)
adjective relating to the management and use of money. *My parents met with a financial advisor to discuss ways to save money for their retirement.*
Spanish cognate: *financiero(a)*

for•mal
(**for**-muhl)
adjective official; not casual. *At the formal dinner, everyone wore fancy clothes.*
Origin: Latin *forma,* meaning "shape, mold"
Spanish cognate: *formal*

fund
(**fuhnd**)
verb to give money to support a plan or a cause. *Several local businesses will fund the town's Independence Day fireworks display.*
Origin: Latin *fundus,* meaning "piece of landed property"

fun•da•men•tal
(fuhn-duh-**men**-tuhl)
adjective basic and necessary. *Being able to read is a fundamental skill in our society.*
Origin: Latin *fundamentum,* meaning "foundation"
Spanish cognate: *fundamental*

gal•ler•y
(**gal**-uh-ree)
noun a place where artworks are displayed and sometimes sold. *The exhibit at the gallery includes some very unusual paintings.*
Spanish cognate: *galería*

gen•e•rate
(**jen**-uh-rate)
verb to create or produce something. *Everyone hopes that the auction will generate a lot of money for the animal shelter.*
Origin: Latin *generat-,* meaning "created"
Spanish cognate: *generar*

gen•er•a•tion
(jen-uh-**ray**-shuhn)
noun all the people who are about the same age. *When my parents were my age, their generation was the first to play video games in a big way.*
Spanish cognate: *generación*

guf•faws
(guh-**fawz**)
noun loud, full laughs. *Grandpa let out several guffaws as he watched the funny movie.*

guide•lines
(**gide**-linez)
noun general rules or advice meant to help you complete a task. *These guidelines will help me create an effective science project.*

gul•ly
(**guhl**-ee)
noun a deep, narrow valley formed by flowing water. *The bridge made it possible for us to cross the gully without getting wet.*

hab•it
(**hab**-it)
noun something a person does regularly, usually without thinking. *Biting your nails is a bad habit.*
Origin: Latin *habitus,* meaning "condition, appearance"

haunt
(**hawnt**)
verb to stay strongly in a person's mind. *Years have passed, but images from the war still haunt the soldier's memory.*

i•den•ti•ty
(eye-**den**-ti-tee)
noun a sense of who you are; a feeling of belonging to a particular group. *My cheerful attitude is a huge part of my personal identity.*
Origin: Latin *idem,* meaning "same"
Spanish cognate: *identidad*

im•pact
(**im**-pakt)
1. *noun* the effect of one thing on another. *The decisions made by the student council have an impact on everyone at school.*
Spanish cognate: *impacto*

2. *verb* to have an effect on someone or something. *Pollution from cars can impact the environment in many ways.*
Spanish cognate: *impactar*
Origin: Latin *impact-,* meaning "driven in" or Latin *impingere,* meaning "drive something in or at"

ACADEMIC GLOSSARY

im•ple•ment
(**im**-pluh-ment)

verb to put a plan or action into effect. *Our principal wants to implement a new rule against bullying.*
Origin: Latin *in-*, meaning "in" + *plere*, meaning "fill"
Spanish cognate: *implementar*

im•prop•er
(im-**prop**-ur)

adjective wrong or not correct. *In our class, it is improper to speak out without raising your hand first.*
Origin: Latin *in-*, meaning "not" + *proprius*, meaning "one's own, special"

in•di•cate
(**in**-duh-kate)

verb to show or point out something. *Those kinds of clouds indicate that stormy weather is on the way.*
Origin: Latin *in-*, meaning "toward" + *dicare*, meaning "make known"
Spanish cognate: *indicar*

in•dus•try
(**in**-duh-stree)

noun a group of related businesses. *Larnelle hopes to work in the advertising industry someday.*
Origin: Latin *industria*, meaning "diligence"
Spanish cognate: *industria*

in•ef•fec•tive
(in-uh-**fek**-tiv)

adjective not successful at achieving the intended result. *The townspeople tried to hold back the floodwaters, but their attempts were ineffective.*
Origin: Latin *in-*, meaning "not" + *efficere*, meaning "accomplish"
Spanish cognate: *ineficaz*

in•flu•ence
(**in**-floo-uhnss)

1. *noun* the power that someone or something has to affect others. *Pop stars often have great influence over the music their fans listen to and buy.*
Spanish cognate: *influencia*

2. *verb* to affect what someone does, says, or believes. *The weather can influence how people dress.*
Spanish cognate: *influenciar, influir en*
Origin: Latin *in-*, meaning "into" + *fluere*, meaning "to flow"

in•for•mal
(in-**for**-muhl)

adjective suitable for everyday or ordinary speech or writing. *When I talk with my friends, I use a more informal tone than when I am speaking to my teacher.*
Origin: Latin *in-*, meaning "not" + *forma*, meaning "shape, mold"
Spanish cognate: *informal*

in•sult
(in-**suhlt**)

verb to say or do something rude or disrespectful. *If you insult your brother by making fun of his mistakes, you should apologize to him.*
Origin: Latin *in-*, meaning "on" + *salire*, meaning "to leap"
Spanish cognate: *insultar*

in•sult•ing
(in-**suhlt**-ing)

adjective rude or disrespectful. *Chris embarrassed Alexis terribly when he made that insulting remark.*
Spanish cognate: *insultante*

in•ter•ac•tive
(in-tur-**ak**-tiv)

adjective referring to technology that allows people to change something or use it to talk to other people. *Many DVDs include games and other interactive features.*
Spanish cognate: *interactivo(a)*

in•ter•pret
(in-**tur**-prit)

verb to determine the meaning of something. *For homework, we will try to interpret the meaning of our favorite poem.*
Origin: Latin *interpres, interpret-,* meaning "agent, translator, interpreter."
Spanish cognate: *interpretar*

in•ter•ven•tion
(in-tur-**ven**-shuhn)

noun an action taken to change a difficult situation. *The riot ended because of direct intervention by the police.*
Origin: Latin *inter-,* meaning "between" + *venire,* meaning "come"
Spanish cognate: *intervención*

is•sue
(**ish**-oo)

noun a topic or problem. *The school board debated the issue of selling junk food in the school cafeteria.*
Origin: Latin *ex-,* meaning "out" + *ire,* meaning "go"

king•dom
(**king**-duhm)

noun one of the main groups into which all living things are divided; a country ruled by a king or queen. *A visit to the zoo will show you just a small part of the animal kingdom. When the prince married his true love, everyone in the kingdom rejoiced.*

le•gal
(**lee**-guhl)

adjective allowed by law. *In our state, it is legal to drive a car if you are over the age of 16.*
Origin: Latin *lex, leg-,* meaning "law"
Spanish cognate: *legal*

leg•is•la•tion
(lej-uh-**slay**-shuhn)

noun a law or group of laws. *The new town legislation does not allow loud music after 9:00 p.m.*
Origin: Latin *lex,* meaning "law" + *latus,* meaning "raised"
Spanish cognate: *legislación*

lit•ter
(**lit**-ur)

verb to leave trash lying around. *We picked up all the garbage from our picnic because it is illegal to litter in the park.*

me•di•um
(**mee**-dee-uhm)

noun a way of communicating information to people. *Through which medium do you watch your favorite shows—television or the Internet?*
Origin: Latin *medius,* meaning "middle"
Spanish cognate: *medio*

mod•er•ate
(**mod**-uh-rate)

verb to make less extreme. *I can moderate my chills with a blanket.*
Origin: Latin *moderat-,* meaning "reduced, controlled"
Spanish cognate: *moderar*

ACADEMIC GLOSSARY

ne•go•ti•ate
(ni-**goh**-shee-ate)
verb to talk about something with someone
else to reach an agreement or a decision.
*Representatives from the warring countries are
meeting to negotiate a peace treaty.*
Origin: Latin *negotium*, meaning "business"
Spanish cognate: *negociar*

norm
(**norm**)
noun an agreed-upon way of behaving
socially. *Most people who live outside of the
accepted norms are looked at as being rather odd.*
Origin: Latin *norma*, meaning "precept, rule,
carpenter's square"
Spanish cognate: *norma*

nu•tri•tion
(noo-**trih**-shuhn)
noun food you need to grow and be healthy.
*Sam takes a vitamin every day to boost his
nutrition.*
Origin: Latin *nutrire*, meaning "feed, nourish"
Spanish cognate: *nutrición*

nu•tri•tion•al
(noo-**trish**-uh-nuhl)
adjective relating to substances you need
to grow and be healthy. *Before she bought the
spaghetti sauce, Monique read the nutritional
information on the label.*
Spanish cognate: *nutritivo(a)*

nu•tri•tious
(noo-**trish**-uhss)
adjective containing substances that your
body can use to help you stay healthy and
strong. *Everyone loved the nutritious foods that
the Thompsons served at their party.*
Spanish cognate: *nutritivo(a)*

o•bese
(oh-**beess**)
adjective so overweight that it is dangerous.
*After years of overeating, my aunt is now obese
and experiencing health problems.*
Origin: Latin *ob-*, meaning "away,
completely" + *esus*, meaning "eaten"
Spanish cognate: *obeso(a)*

o•be•si•ty
(oh-**beess**-ih-tee)
noun the condition of being so overweight
that it is dangerous. *Too much fast food can
lead to obesity.*
Spanish cognate: *obesidad*

oc•cur
(uh-**kur**)
verb to take place or happen. *Fire drills occur
twice per month at our school.*
Origin: Latin *occurrere*, meaning "go to meet,
present itself"
Spanish cognate: *ocurrir*

of•fend•ers
(uh-**fen**-durz)
noun people who commit crimes or cause
other kinds of trouble. *Police arrested the
offenders and took them in for questioning.*
Origin: Latin *offendere*, meaning "strike
against"

on the rise
(on the **rize**)
adjective increasing; becoming more
widespread. *Thanks to a larger police force,
crime in our community is no longer on the rise.*

op•ti•mize
(**op**-tuh-mize)
verb to make something as good or helpful
as possible. *You should exercise to optimize
your health.*
Origin: Latin *optimus,* meaning "best" + *-ize*
Spanish cognate: *optimizar*

op•tions
(**op**-shuhnz)
noun choices that someone can make about
a particular situation. *I looked at all of the
options before I decided to have pizza for lunch.*
Origin: Latin *optare,* meaning "choose"
Spanish cognate: *opciones*

po•lit•i•cal
(puh-**lit**-i-kuhl)
adjective having to do with governments
and how they are run. *The presidential
candidates debated the political issues they most
cared about.*
Origin: Greek *polis,* meaning "city"
Spanish cognate: *político(a)*

pol•lute
(puh-**loot**)
verb to use harmful materials that damage
or contaminate the air, water, and soil. *The oil
spill taught me about the damage that occurs
when people pollute the ocean.*
Origin: Latin *pollut-,* meaning "soiled, defiled"

pol•lu•tion
(puh-**loo**-shuhn)
noun harmful materials that damage or
contaminate the air, water, and soil. *Exhaust
from cars can cause air pollution.*

po•ten•tial
(puh-**ten**-shuhl)
1. *noun* the chance of something happening.
*This new invention has enormous potential to
change the way that people communicate.*

2. *adjective* a way of expressing possibility.
*Since my neighbor has three dogs, he is a
potential customer for my dog-walking business.*
Origin: Latin *potentialis,* meaning "power"
Spanish cognate: *potencial*

pred•a•tor
(**pred**-uh-tur)
noun an animal that kills other animals for
food. *The hungry lion, a predator, silently
stalked the herd of antelope.*
Origin: Latin *praedat-,* meaning
"seized as plunder"
Spanish cognate: *predador*

prev•a•lent
(**pre**-vuh-luhnt)
adjective common or widespread. *Identity
theft is a prevalent fear in society today.*
Origin: Latin *praevalent-,* meaning "having
greater power"
Spanish cognate: *prevalente*

pre•vent
(pri-**vent**)
verb to stop something from happening.
Brushing your teeth can help prevent cavities.
Origin: Latin *prae,* meaning "before" + *venire,*
meaning "come"
Spanish cognate: *prevenir*

pre•ven•tion
(pri-**vent**-shuhn)
noun the act of stopping something from
happening. *During Fire Prevention Week, we
learned how to put out different kinds of fires.*
Spanish cognate: *prevención*

ACADEMIC GLOSSARY

pri•or•i•ty
(prye-**or**-uh-tee)
noun something that is more important than other things. *Of all the things he could do this weekend, Alan's priority is going to his school's basketball game.*
Origin: Latin *prioritas,* meaning "former"
Spanish cognate: prioridad

pro•duce
(pruh-**dooss**)
verb to create something new. *We hope that medical research will produce a cure for cancer in our lifetime.*
Origin: Latin *pro-,* meaning "forward" + *ducere,* meaning "to lead"
Spanish cognate: producir

pro•duc•tion
(pruh-**duhk**-shuhn)
noun the process of creating new things. *The new model was so popular that the automobile company increased its production.*
Spanish cognate: producción

prop•er
(**prop**-ur)
adjective correct or appropriate for a situation. *Colton showed us the proper way to tie a square knot.*
Origin: Latin *proprius,* meaning "one's own, special"

re•as•sess
(ree-uh-**sess**)
verb to think about something again in order to change your way of thinking. *Information presented in the new report caused the committee to reassess its plans.*
Origin: Latin *re-,* meaning "again" + *ad-,* meaning "to, at" + *sedere,* meaning "sit"

reck•on
(**rek**-uhn)
verb to think or have an opinion. *It's raining now, but I reckon that the sun will be out by the time we have to leave.*

re•cy•cle
(ree-**sye**-kuhl)
verb to put used objects through a process so they can be made into something new. *Our school has special containers so that we can recycle bottles, cans, and paper.*
Origin: Latin *re-,* meaning "again" + Greek *kuklos,* meaning "circle" or "circular motion"
Spanish cognate: reciclar

re•flec•tion
(ree-**flek**-shuhn)
noun an accurate way of showing something. *Joey's frequent smiles are a reflection of his cheerful personality.*
Origin: Latin *reflex-,* meaning "bent back"
Spanish cognate: reflejo

re•late
(ri-**late**)
verb to connect. *The poems that we are writing in class all relate to important moments in American history.*
Origin: Latin *relat-,* meaning "brought back"
Spanish cognate: relacionar

re•lat•ed
(ri-**lay**-tid)
adjective having a connection. *Fernando and Catalina are related; in fact, they are cousins.*
Spanish cognate: relacionado(a)

re·la·tion
(ri-**lay**-shuhn)
noun a connection. *What is the relation between the amount of sleep you get and your overall health?*
Spanish cognate: *relación*

re·la·tion·ship
(ri-**lay**-shuhn-ship)
noun the way that people feel about and behave toward each other. *Dad often speaks of his good relationship with the people at his workplace.*
Spanish cognate: *relación*

rel·e·vant
(**rel**-uh-vuhnt)
adjective directly relating to an issue or matter. *Steven checked out all the books that were relevant to his report on sea turtles.*
Origin: Latin *relevant-,* meaning "raising up"
Spanish cognate: *relevante*

re·mov·al
(ri-**moov**-uhl)
noun the act of taking something away. *At home, removal of the trash is my responsibility.*

re·move
(ri-**moov**)
verb to take something away. *Before we install the new carpet, we will temporarily remove the furniture from the living room.*
Origin: Latin *re-,* meaning "back" + *movere,* meaning "to move"

rep·re·sent
(rep-ri-**zent**)
verb to be a sign or mark that means something. *Maps use symbols to visually represent things like roads, oceans, and hotels.*
Origin: Latin *repraesentare,* meaning "to present"
Spanish cognate: *representar*

re·source
(**ree**-sorss)
noun available land, water, and natural energy that can be used; something used to make life easier. *Coal is a useful resource for the people who use it to heat their houses.*
Origin: Latin *re-,* meaning "again" + *surgere,* meaning "to rise"
Spanish cognate: *recurso*

re·strict
(ri-**strikt**)
verb to limit the size, amount, or range of something. *My mom restricts the amount of time I spend on the computer.*
Origin: Latin *re-,* meaning "back" + *stringere,* meaning "to tie, pull tight"
Spanish cognate: *restringir*

re·tail·ers
(**ree**-tay-lurz)
noun people or businesses who sell products to customers. *Some major retailers offer discounts if you buy a number of the same item.*

re·us·a·ble
(ree-**yoo**-zuh-buhl)
adjective capable of being used more than once. *Reusable bags help protect the environment because they don't create more trash.*

ACADEMIC GLOSSARY

re•use
(ree-**yooz**)

verb to use something more than once. *Instead of throwing out that plastic bin, wash it so that we can reuse it.*
Origin: Latin *re-*, meaning "again" + *uti*, meaning "to use"

role
(**rohl**)

noun the way in which someone or something is involved in an activity or situation. *My grandfather has played an important role in teaching me about football.*

rul•ers
(**roo**-lurz)

noun those who have power over people or places. *In a matriarchy, women are the rulers over their families or tribes.*
Origin: Latin *regere*, meaning "to rule, straighten, guide"

se•lect
(si-**lekt**)

verb to pick out or choose. *Every morning I carefully select a shirt to wear.*
Origin: Latin *se-*, meaning "apart" + *legere*, meaning "choose"
Spanish cognate: *seleccionar*

short•cuts
(**short**-kuhtz)

noun faster, simpler ways of doing things. *If you want to save a document on the computer, you can use various shortcuts on the keyboard.*

so•cial
(**soh**-shuhl)

adjective having to do with the way people spend time with other people. *I enjoy going to parties, concerts, and other social events.*
Origin: Latin *socius,* meaning "friend"
Spanish cognate: *social*

so•journ•ers
(**soh**-jur-nuhrz)

noun travelers; people who stay in one place for only a short time. *When my cousins traveled the country last summer, those sojourners stayed with us for two days before moving on.*

stig•ma
(**stig**-ma)

noun a mark of shame or embarrassment. *Even after they apologized, the students who had cheated felt a stigma because of what they had done.*
Origin: Greek *stigma,* meaning "a mark made by a pointed instrument"
Spanish cognate: *estigma*

strong•hold
(**strong**-hohld)

noun a place that is protected against attack or danger. *The walls of the ancient city made it a stronghold for the people who lived there.*

sup•port
(suh-**port**)

verb to agree with something or someone. *Most students at my school enthusiastically support our sports teams.*
Origin: Latin *sub-,* meaning "from below" + *portare*, meaning "carry"

sup•port•er
(suh-**por**-tur)
noun a person who believes in someone or favors something. *Mrs. Edwards is a loyal supporter of the mayor, who is running for a second term.*

sur•vey
(**sur**-vay)
noun the act of asking people the same questions to find out their opinions or behavior. *The results of our survey show that students prefer a later lunch period.*
Origin: Latin *super,* meaning "over," + *videre,* meaning "see"

tar•get
(**tar**-git)
noun someone or someplace that becomes the focus of an action or an activity, especially in a negative way. *The senator's questionable investments made him the target of an investigation.*

tax
(**taks**)
noun money paid to the government for public services, such as education and roads. *The increase in the local property tax will help pay for school improvements.*
Origin: Latin *taxare,* meaning "to evaluate" or "to charge"

tech•ni•cal
(**tek**-nuh-kuhl)
adjective related to machines, science, or computers. *Chandra's technical skills make her the perfect person to show me how to use my new tablet.*
Spanish cognate: técnico(a)

tech•ni•cal•ly
(**tek**-nuh-kuhl-ee)
adverb actually or really, but not in the way that some people think about it. *Even though Luke is technically old enough to get his learner's permit, he isn't eager to start driving.*
Origin: Greek *tekhnē,* meaning "art"

tech•nol•o•gy
(tek-**nol**-uh-jee)
noun the use of science and computers to do everyday tasks. *I don't know how my parents grew up without the advances in technology that we have today.*
Origin: Greek *tekhnē,* meaning "art, craft" + *-logia,* meaning "study of"
Spanish cognate: tecnología

tox•ic
(**tok**-sik)
adjective containing poison. *It is important to store toxic material where young children and pets can't reach it.*
Origin: Greek *toxikon,* meaning "arrow poison"
Spanish cognate: tóxico(a)

trend
(**trend**)
noun a general direction in which a situation is changing. *Getting an education through an online school is a growing trend.*

u•biq•ui•tous
(yoo-**bih**-kwuh-tuss)
adjective found everywhere. *That ubiquitous song is showing up in movies, TV shows, and commercials.*
Origin: Latin *ubique,* meaning "everywhere"
Spanish cognate: ubicuo(a)

un•der•mined
(**uhn**-dur-mined)

verb weakened or destroyed something slowly. *Gossip and lies undermined the candidate's chances to be elected.*

un•di•vid•ed at•ten•tion
(uhn-duh-**vide**-id uh-ten-shuhn)

noun phrase careful thought that is not interrupted by thinking about something else. *Because the speakers at the assembly were very interesting, they had everyone's undivided attention.*

val•i•dat•ing
(**val**-uh-day-ting)

adjective proving the value or correctness of something. *When the coach praises the team, it's a validating moment for everyone.*
Origin: Latin *validus,* meaning "strong"
Spanish cognate: *validado(a)*

van•dal
(**van**-duhl)

noun someone who purposely damages property. *Have the police caught the vandal who sprayed graffiti all over the town hall?*
Spanish cognate: *vándalo*

van•dal•ism
(**van**-duhl-izm)

noun the act of purposely destroying or damaging the way something looks, especially public property. *You will be automatically suspended if you commit any act of vandalism at school.*
Spanish cognate: *vandalismo*

ver•sion
(**vur**-zhuhn)

noun a different or changed form of something. *The Cinderella story we know may be a European version of an ancient story from China.*
Origin: Latin *vertere,* meaning "to turn"
Spanish cognate: *versión*

vic•tim•less
(**vik**-tuhm-liss)

adjective without anyone being injured or harmed. *Gambling is called a victimless crime, but I think that it hurts the gambler at least.*
Spanish cognate: *sin víctimas*

vi•o•lence
(**vye**-uh-luhnss)

noun the use of great force or strength in a destructive way. *With so many crime shows, I see more acts of violence on TV than I do in real life.*
Origin: Latin *violent-,* meaning "vehement, violent"
Spanish cognate: *violencia*

vi•o•lent
(**vye**-uh-luhnt)

adjective involving actions that are likely to hurt or kill other people. *The weather report warned that a very violent storm would hit our town this evening.*
Spanish cognate: *violento(a)*

Issue 1: Gaming

Armstrong Moore, Elizabeth. "New Study Links Video Gaming to Creativity." *CNET.* CBS Interactive, 2 Nov. 2011. Web. 17 Feb. 2015. <http://www.cnet.com/news/new-study-links-video-gaming-to-creativity/>.

Entertainment Software Association. *2014 Essential Facts About the Computer and Video Game Industry.* Entertainment Software Association, 2014. Web. 17 Feb. 2015. <http://www.theesa.com/wp-content/uploads/2014/11/ESA-Media-Resources.zip>.

Gable, Lawrence. "The Supreme Court Looks at Violent Video Games." *What's Happening in the USA?* 18.7 (2011): 2. Print.

Gentile, Douglas. "Pathological Video-Game Use Among Youth Ages 8 to 18." *Psychological Science* 20.5 (2009): 594–602. Print. <http://drdouglas.org/drdpdfs/Gentile_Pathological_VG_Use_2009e.pdf>.

Gomez, Oscar. "Game On or Game Over?" *Issues.* Vol. 1. New York: Houghton Mifflin Harcourt, 2016. 6–11. Print.

Lenhart, Amanda, et al. *Teens, Video Games, and Civics.* Washington: Pew Internet & American Life Project, 16 Sept. 2008. Web. 17 Feb. 2015. <http://www.pewinternet.org/files/old-media//Files/Reports/2008/PIP_Teens_Games_and_Civics_Report_FINAL.pdf.pdf>.

Issue 2: Healthy Choices

American Heart Association. "What Is Childhood Obesity?" *Getting Healthy: Healthier Kids.* American Heart Association, Aug. 2014. Web. 17 Feb. 2015. <http://www.heart.org/HEARTORG/GettingHealthy/HealthierKids/ChildhoodObesity/What-is-childhood-obesity_UCM_304347_Article.jsp>.

Gable, Lawrence. "Food Packages Get Improved Information." *What's Happening in the USA?* 21.8 (2014): 2. Print.

Obama, Michelle. "Remarks by the First Lady at a Let's Move! School Wellness Standards Announcement." The White House, Washington. 25 Feb. 2014. Address. <http://www.whitehouse.gov/photos-and-video/video/2014/02/25/first-lady-announces-new-school-wellness-standards#transcript>.

Obama, Michelle. "The First Lady Announces New School Wellness Standards." Online video clip. *whitehouse.gov.* The White House, 25 Feb. 2014. Web. 17 Feb. 2015. <http://www.whitehouse.gov/photos-and-video/video/2014/02/25/first-lady-announces-new-school-wellness-standards>.

Rodriguez, Dora. "Food Fight." *Issues.* Vol. 1. New York: Houghton Mifflin Harcourt, 2016. 16–20. Print.

SOURCES

Thompson, Olivia M., et al. "School Vending Machine Purchasing Behavior: Results From the 2005 YouthStyles Survey." *Journal of School Health*. 80.5 (2010): 225–232. Print.

United States. Dept. of Agriculture. Center for Nutrition Policy and Promotion. *MyPlate*. 2010. Center for Nutrition Policy and Promotion. Web. 17 Feb. 2015. <http://www.choosemyplate.gov/print-materials-ordering/graphic-resources.html>.

United States. Dept. of Agriculture. Food and Nutrition Service. *Program Information Report (Keydata)*. Food and Nutrition Service, Mar. 2014. Web. 17 Feb. 2015. <http://www.fns.usda.gov/sites/default/files/datastatistics/Keydata-March-2014_0.pdf>.

Issue 3: Street Art

California Penal Code § 594

"Fast Facts About Graffiti." *Graffiti Hurts*. Keep America Beautiful, Inc., 2014. Web. 17 Feb. 2015. <http://www.graffitihurts.org/getfacts/fastfacts.jsp>.

Florida Statute § 806.13

"Graffiti." *San Francisco Public Works*. City and County of San Francisco, n.d. Web. 17 Feb. 2015. <http://www.sfdpw.org/index.aspx?page=1099>.

Kabwato, Ethel Irene. "Graffiti on Christina Street." *Poetry International*. Poetry International, 2013. Web. 17 Feb. 2015. <http://www.poetryinternationalweb.net/pi/site/poem/item/23129/auto/GRAFFITI-ON-CHRISTINA-STREET>.

New York Penal Law § 145.00

Nguyen, Kim. "The Writing on the Wall." *Issues*. Vol. 1. New York: Houghton Mifflin Harcourt, 2011. 23–27. Print.

"Spirit of the Streets." *New York Times*. New York Times, 29 Aug. 2013. Web. 17 Feb. 2015. <http://www.nytimes.com/slideshow/2013/08/30/arts/design/20130830-STREETS.html?ref=design&_r=0>.

Texas Penal Code § 28.03

Weisel, Deborah Lamm. *Graffiti*. Washington: U.S. Dept. of Justice, Office of Community Oriented Policing Services, 2009. Web. 17 Feb. 2015. <http://ric-zai-inc.com/Publications/cops-p026-pub.pdf>.

"Who Owns Street Art?" *Scholastic Art*. Apr.–May 2011: 12. Print.

Wu, Tim. "Is There 'Hope' for Shepard Fairey?" *Slate*. The Slate Group LLC, 21 Oct. 2009. Web. 17 Feb. 2015. <http://www.slate.com/articles/news_and_politics/jurisprudence/2009/10/is_there_hope_for_shepard_fairey.html>.

Issue 4: Plastic Pollution

"5 Gyres Institute: Exhibit Video." *Vimeo*. Ed. 5 Gyres Institute. 5 Gyres Institute, 26 Mar. 2013. Web. 13 Feb. 2015. <http://vimeo.com/62675237>.

Allsopp, Michelle, Adam Walters, David Santillo, and Paul Johnston. "Plastic Debris in the World's Oceans." *Greenpeace* (2006): 6. Web. 17 Feb. 2015. <http://www.greenpeace.org/international/Global/international/planet-2/report/2007/8/plastic_ocean_report.pdf>.

Gable, Lawrence. "Local Governments Ban Plastic Bags." *What's Happening in California?* 12.5 (2011): 1. Print.

Larsen, Janet, and Savina Venkova. "Plan B Updates: The Downfall of the Plastic Bag: A Global Picture." *Earth Policy Institute*. N.p., 1 May 2014. Web. 16 Feb. 2015. <http://www.earth-policy.org/plan_b_updates/2014/update123>.

Larsen, Janet, and Savina Venkova. "Plan B Updates: Plastic Bag Bans Spreading in the United States." *Earth Policy Institute*. N.p., 22 Apr. 2014. Web. 17 Feb. 2015. <http://www.earth-policy.org/plan_b_updates/2014/update122>.

Lynn, Hasselberger. "22 Facts About Plastic Pollution (And 10 Things We Can Do About It)." *EcoWatch*. N.p., 7 Apr. 2014. Web. 11 Feb. 2015. <http://ecowatch.com/2014/04/07/22-facts-plastic-pollution-10-things-can-do-about-it/>.

Malik, Sanjay. "Ban It or Bag It?" *Issues*. Vol. 1. New York: Houghton Mifflin Harcourt, 2016. 41–45. Print.

Parker, Laura. "With Millions of Tons of Plastic in Oceans, More Scientists Studying Impact." *National Geographic*. National Geographic Society, 13 June 2014. Web. 13 Feb. 2015. <http://news.nationalgeographic.com/news/2014/06/140613-ocean-trash-garbage-patch-plastic-science-kerry-marine-debris/>.

United States. Environmental Protection Agency. *Municipal Solid Waste Generation, Recycling, and Disposal in the United States: Facts and Figures for 2012*. EPA, Feb. 2014. Web. 17 Feb. 2015. <http://www.epa.gov/solidwaste/nonhaz/municipal/pubs/2012_msw_fs.pdf>.

Wong, Kristine. "Bye-Bye, Bags and Bottles: This Woman Lives Plastic-Free." *TakePart*. Participant Media, 23 Apr. 2014. Web. 13 Feb. 2015. <http://www.takepart.com/article/2014/04/22/were-living-material-world-woman-proved-its-possible-go-plastic-free>.

SOURCES

Issue 5: Texting

"BFF, n." OED Online. Oxford University Press, Dec. 2014. Web. 18 Feb. 2015.

"Crisis Texting With Bob Filbin." *Spark*. Host Nora Young. CBC, 3 Oct. 2014. *CBC.ca*. Web. 17 Feb. 2015. <http://www.cbc.ca/radio/spark/crisis-texting-with-bob-filbin-1.2582202>.

Filbin, Bob. "Crisis Trends." *Crisis Text Line*. Crisis Text Line, n.d. Web. 12 Mar. 2015. <http://www.crisistextline.org/trends/>.

Fisher, Ken. "LOL, Texting, and Txt-speak: Linguistic Miracles." *Ars Technica*. Conde Nast, 28 Feb. 2013. Web. 17 Feb. 2015. <http://arstechnica.com/science/2013/02/lol-texting-and-txt-speak-linguistic-miracles/>.

"Frequently Asked Questions About the Mobile Giving Foundation." *Mobile Giving Foundation*. Mobile Giving Foundation, n.d. Web. 12 Mar. 2015. <http://mobilegiving.org/?page_id=24>.

"FYI, phr., adj., and n." OED Online. Oxford University Press, Dec. 2014. Web. 18 Feb. 2015.

Hafner, Katie. "Is 2 Much Txtng Bad 4 U?." *New York Times Upfront* 5 Oct. 2009: 20. Print.

Kaufman, Leslie. "In Texting Era, Crisis Hotlines Put Help at Youths' Fingertips." *New York Times*. New York Times, 4 Feb. 2014. Web. 17 Feb. 2015. <http://www.nytimes.com/2014/02/05/us/in-texting-era-crisis-hotlines-put-help-at-youths-fingertips.html?_r=1>.

McGann, Laura. "Attention Nonprofits: Young Adults Love Texting Donations." *NiemanLab*. Harvard, 7 July 2010. Web. 12 Mar. 2015. <http://www.niemanlab.org/2010/07/attention-nonprofits-young-adults-love-texting-donations>.

"OMG, int. (and n.) and adj." OED Online. Oxford University Press, Dec. 2014. Web. 18 Feb. 2015.

Lenhart, Amanda. *Teens, Smartphones & Texting*. Pew Research Center, 19 Mar. 2012. Web. 12 Mar. 2015 < http://www.pewinternet.org/files/old-media//Files/Reports/2012/PIP_Teens_Smartphones_and_Texting.pdf>.

"LOL, int. and n.2." OED Online. Oxford University Press, Dec. 2014. Web. 18 Feb. 2015.

Smith, Natalie. "luv 2 txt." *Scholastic Choices,* Sept. 2010: 12–14. Print.

United States. Federal Communications Commission. *Second Report and Order and Third Further Notice of Proposed Rulemaking*. Federal Communications Commission. 13 Aug. 2014. Web. 12 Mar. 2015. <https://apps.fcc.gov/edocs_public/attachmatch/FCC-14-118A1.pdf>.

"U.S. Teen Mobile Report Calling Yesterday, Texting Today, Using Apps Tomorrow."
    Newswire. Nielsen, 14 Oct. 2010. Web. 12 Mar. 2015. <http://
    www.nielsen.com/us/en/insights/news/2010/
    u-s-teen-mobile-report-calling-yesterday-texting-today-using-apps-tomorrow.html>.

Issue 6: Fast Friends

Ahlberg, Allan, and Fritz Wegner. "It's a Puzzle." *Please Mrs Butler*. Harmondsworth:
    Puffin, 1984. 40. Print.

Cisneros, Sandra. "Our Good Day." *The House on Mango Street*. New York: Vintage,
    1991. 14–16. Print.

Paterson, Katherine, Steve Liebman, and Stephanie S. Tolan. *Bridge to Terabithia:
    A Play With Music*. New York: Samuel French, 1992. 24–37. Print.

Paterson, Katherine. *Bridge to Terabithia*. New York: HarperTeen, 2004. *Bridge to
    Terabithia by Katherine Paterson, Part 2. Scholastic*, n.d. Web. 17 Feb. 2015.
    <http://www.scholastic.com/browse/article.jsp?id=3751208>.

CREDITS

Grateful acknowledgment is made to the following sources for permission to reprint from previously published material. The publisher has made diligent efforts to trace the ownership of all copyrighted material in this volume and believes that all necessary permissions have been secured. If any errors or omissions have inadvertently been made, proper corrections will gladly be made in future editions.

ISSUE 1: GAMING

"New Study Links Video Gaming to Creativity" by Elizabeth Armstrong Moore from the CNET website. Copyright © 2011 by CBS Interactive Inc. Used by permission of CBS Interactive Inc.

ISSUE 3: STREET ART

"Graffiti on Christina Street" by Ethel Irene Kabwato from the Poetry International website. Copyright © 2013 by Ethel Irene Kabwato. Reprinted by permission of the author.

ISSUE 4: PLASTIC POLLUTION

"With Millions of Tons of Plastic in Oceans, More Scientists Studying Impact" by Laura Parker from the National Geographic website. Copyright © 2014 by National Geographic Society. Used by permission of National Geographic Society.

"Bye-Bye, Bags and Bottles" by Kristine Wong from www.takepart.com. Copyright © 2014 by TakePart, LLC. Used by permission of TakePart, LLC.

ISSUE 5: TEXTING

"luv 2 txt" by Natalie Smith from *Scholastic Choices* magazine, September 2010. Copyright © 2010 by Scholastic Inc. All rights reserved.

"LOL, Texting, and Txt-Speak: Linguistic Miracles" by Ken Fisher from the Ars Technica website, February 28, 2013. Copyright © 2013 by Condé Nast Publications. Used by permission.

"In Texting Era, Crisis Hotlines Put Help at Youths' Fingertips" by Leslie Kaufman from the New York Times website, February 4, 2014. Copyright © 2014 by The New York Times Company. Used by permission.

ISSUE 6: FAST FRIENDS

From "Bridge to Terabithia: A Play With Music" by Katherine Paterson and Stephanie Tolan. Copyright © 1992 by Katherine Paterson and Stephanie Tolan. Used by permission of Susan Schulman Literary Agency.

From *The House on Mango Street* by Sandra Cisneros. Copyright © 1984 by Sandra Cisneros. Published by Vintage Books, a division of Penguin Random House, and in hardcover by Alfred E. Knopf in 1994. By permission of Susan Bergholz Literary Services, New York, NY and Lamy, NM, and Bloomsbury Publishing PLC. All rights reserved.

Front Cover (bl) ©Soleilc/Dreamstime; p. 2 (b) © Jupiterimages/Thinkstock; p. 2 (t) ©Bruce Rolff/ Shutterstock; p. 2 (c) ©Sinisa Bobic/Shutterstock; p. 2 (bg) ©koteik/Shutterstock; p. 3 (b) ©Peter Coombs Photography; p. 3 (t) ©Cheryl Ravelo/Reuters; p. 3 (tl) ©Fabian Monteil/Dreamstime; p. 4 (t) ©Bruce Rolff/Shutterstock; pp. 6–13 (bg) ©simon2579/DigitalVisionVectors/Getty Images; pp. 6–7 (br) ©JGI/Blend Images/Media Bakery; p. 7 (br) ©PA2 Jennifer Johnson/U.S. Coast Guard; p. 8 (b) ©BSIP/Science Source; p. 9 (b) ©Kwame Zikomo/Media Bakery; p. 10 (t) ©Olivier Douliery/ Abaca Press/MCT via Newscom; pp. 12–13 (b) ©Verkoka/Dreamstime; p. 13 (tr) ©Monkey Business Images/Shutterstock; p. 14 (bg) ©Robert Gubbins/Adobe Stock; p. 15 (tl) ©Ihorzigor/Dreamstime; p. 15 (cl) ©Aliaksandra Molash/Dreamstime; p. 15 (bl) ©Pavel Strezhnev/Dreamstime; p. 16 (br) ©Sinisa Bobic/Shutterstock; p. 18 (b) ©Center for Nutrition Policy and Promotion/U.S. Dept of Agriculture USDA Photography Center; p. 19 (t) ©Emily Rasinski/St. Louis Post Disptach/MCT/Newscom; p. 22 (b) Courtesy Barack Obama Presidential Library; p. 23 (tr) ©Rick E. Martin/San Jose Mercury News via Newscom; p. 24 (br) ©Jupiterimages/Getty Images; p. 24 (bg) ©koteik/Shutterstock; p. 25 (tl) ©AlonzoDesign/DigitalVisionVectors/Getty Images; p. 26 (b) © Bebeto Mattthews/AP Images; p. 26 (bg) ©koteik/Shutterstock; p. 29 (b) ©Walter Bibikow/Danita Delimont Stock Photography; p. 30 (b) ©Carlos Chavarria/Redux Pictures; p. 31 (br) ©Geoff Hargadon/Obey Giant Art Inc; pp. 32–33 (bg) ©Capsule/iStockphoto/Getty Images Plus; p. 33 bl: photo by B. Leon courtesy of Ethel Kabwato; pp. 34–35 (bg) ©Patricia Danna/Biosphoto; p. 34 (c) ©Poprugin Aleksey/Shutterstock; p. 35 (cl) © Er Ten Hong/Getty Images; p. 35 (tl) © Soleilc/Dreamstime; p. 35 (c) © Poprugin Aleksey/Shutterstock; p. 36 ©Paulo Oliveira/Alamy; p. 38 (tl) ©Asasirov/Shutterstock; p. 38 (bl) ©Design56/Dreamstime; p. 38 (c) ©Poprugin Aleksey/Shutterstock; p. 39 (tr) ©Christopher Robbins/Photoplay/Media Bakery; p. 40 (cr) ©Cheryl Ravelo/Reuters; p. 42 ©Fabian Monteil/Dreamstime; p. 43 (tr) ©Reed Saxon/AP Images; p. 44 (b) ©Dr. Dwayne Meadows, NOAA/NMFS/OPR; p. 45 ©Stephen Loewinsohn Photography; p. 47 (t) ©Ariel Skelley/Digital Vision/Getty Images; p. 50 ©amana Images Inc./Getty Images; p. 53 ©kimberrywood/Shutterstock; p. 54 (br) ©Alex Wong/Getty Images for Meet the Press; p. 55 (cr) ©Neirfy/Adobe Stock; p. 57 (b) ©denys_kuvaiev/Adobe Stock; p. 59 (br) ©Thomas Concordia/Getty Images for Rock Art Love; p. 61 (cr) ©Dcarto/Dreamstime; p. 62 (r) ©Peter Coombs Photography; p. 72 (b) ©Jahi Chikwendiu/The Washington Post via Getty Images; p. 74 (t) ©Peter Coombs Photography; p. 75 ©Robert McLeroy/San Antonio Express/Zuma Press; All other photos ©Houghton Mifflin Harcourt.